MUSCAT COMMAND

MUSCAT COMMAND

by
PETER THWAITES

completed by
SIMON SLOANE

LEO COOPER
LONDON

This book is dedicated to Peter's children, Allegra, Christian and Grania, who were constantly in his thoughts during the Dhofar campaign, and to whom he was absolutely devoted.

First published in Great Britain in 1995 by
LEO COOPER
an imprint of
Pen & Sword Ltd
47 Church Street, Barnsley, South Yorks S70 2AS

© Executors of the late Peter Thwaites and
Simon Sloane, 1995

A CIP catalogue record for this book is available
from the British Library

ISBN 0 85052 411 3

Printed by
Redwood Books Ltd
Trowbridge, Wiltshire

FOREWORD

by
Major-General The Duke of Norfolk,
KG, GCVO, CB, CBE, MC, DL

Those Grenadiers who served with Peter Thwaites will always recall his energy and efficiency. His direct and sometimes irascible manner was balanced by a mischievous sense of humour and an unquestionable thirst for adventure. As a young subaltern he found being stationed at Windsor boring and even Germany tedious and unexciting.

Peter's elder brother, Tommy, was killed with the 5th Battalion at the Battle of Bagnoregio but Peter himself missed the war, joining the regiment in 1944 in the last intake before D Day.

His successful career was eventful in the military sense, but the genes of a literary family background were evidenced in his continual writings of both books and plays.

Although he was a peacetime soldier, he served in two theatres of terrorism if not outright war. He was a Brigade Major in the Malayan emergency, before taking command of the Muscat Regiment in Oman. "Sounds good," he remarked laconically when the appointment was suggested, and off he went to serve the Sultan, Said bin Taimur, in the savage terrain of Dhofar.

This was certainly the most exciting chapter of his varied career. In Oman he was responsible for several dangerous operations which incurred casualties on both sides. For this he was awarded the Sultan's Bravery Medal, the Special Commendation and Oman's Distinguished Service Medal for Gallantry. He served two Sultans, refusing to associate the Muscat Regiment with the overthrow of the old Sultan, whose friend he remained until he died in exile in 1969.

In 1977, after a period at the Ministry of Defence and time spent on the Staff in Singapore, he agreed to return to head the staff of the Armed Forces of Sultan Qaboos, as a Brigadier and Chairman of the Joint Staff of Oman.

Born at Ambleside in Westmorland in the house of his godfather, Gordon Wordsworth, he was educated at Rugby, the school made famous by his great-great-grandfather, Dr Arnold. His literary success was confined to light plays, his military commitments allowing little time for him to develop fully as a writer. Nevertheless he wrote whenever and wherever he could, and this constant application has much to do with the crisp spontaneous style that is evident in this account of this time in Oman.

He was a successful sportsman, riding and winning races in Germany for the Regiment, captaining the regimental polo team, chairing the Household Brigade Polo Club and finally, in his retirement, becoming chairman of the ruling body of polo, the Hurlingham Polo Association. He has been described as a notably versatile officer. He was certainly a creative thinker in adversity, a fine sportsman, a talented writer and a most charming and gregarious colleague and friend.

Miles Norfolk.   16 December 1994

ACKNOWLEDGEMENTS

My late husband, Peter Thwaites, died before he was able to complete this book and it is thus left to myself to thank all those who have contributed to his work both during and after his lifetime.

The period of which he writes occurred before our marriage in 1974 but he spoke to me often of the days in Dhofar: in 1977 he returned to Oman as chairman of the Joint Staff, serving His Majesty Sultan Qaboos bin Said al Taimur in that capacity for four years. Thus, I, too, went to Oman and made frequent visits to Salalah with him. We travelled together on the jebel and flew over the daunting terrain where the war he describes so vividly was fought with determination and much difficulty. Always he expressed the greatest regard for his officers. The effort of coping with this "forgotten war", with inadequate and often inferior weaponry, in a climate unsympathetic to the Western physique, was constantly ameliorated in his mind then, and later in his memory, by the support, the dedication and the humour of those young men who came from the British Services to join the Muscat Regiment and risk their lives to counter the advances of subversion. I know that he would wish to acknowledge this, to reaffirm to them that they made his problems easier to cope with, that their comradeship and loyalty was of inestimable value to him at the time, and in retrospect was a source of both pride and pleasure.

Because I have met most of these officers I can add my gratitude to Peter's: it is not so easy for me to identify the Omani and Baluchi soldiers who served in the Regiment with courage and devotion. I must, however, express my personal thanks to the intrepid Dad Karim, who went into action regularly laden with an extra burden of water, so that Peter should not suffer unduly from his faulty kidneys. Peter often told me that Dad Karim's water saved his life and I know that, among the many serving soldiers, Dad Karim was always remembered with special gratitude.

Patrick Brook was frequently singled out in his reminiscences as a "wonderful adjutant, absolutely tireless". I suspect that the forty-year-old Colonel, determined not to give in to ill health, had much reason to be grateful to Patrick and others close to him for far more than the disciplined reliability expected of a British officer.

Initially Peter typed his own manuscript, two or three fingers being all that he could call into play! Eventually he reverted to script and each chapter was typed by Mrs R. M. Duke-Wooley, checked and retyped with infinite patience. The last chapter was still in draft when he died and even I could barely read the writing, once so elegant, now marred by the effects of fatigue and his anxiety to hurry, to finish before he was overtaken by death. "Don't worry," I was told, "I know the writing so well now, I will manage," and so she did; I was and remain so very grateful to her.

Alas, the book was still unfinished. The narrative needed an ending, and it was Peter's intention to review the effect of the Dhofar victory and the dramatic social developments which have subsequently taken place under Sultan Qaboos. In the event Simon Sloane, his first Adjutant who subsequently commanded C Company for two years under Peter's command, most kindly volunteered to write the last three chapters and this he has done. I am immensely grateful that his work has brought Peter's book to publication and I know that Peter would be the first to acknowledge this kindnesss, and to thank him personnally.

Finally, my own thanks are due to those kind friends who have searched through their papers for precious photographs of the campaign. Ranulph Fiennes, Simon Sloane, David Bayley, Richard John and Guy Sheridan have all generously contributed to the few pictorial records that Peter took himself. I hope they will add interest for those readers who have not visited this magical country, a country that has a long association with Great Britain and whose interests were so well worth defending against the threat of communism.

Jacqueline Duncan
9 November, 1994

INTRODUCTION

by
Simon Sloane

In 1967 Peter Thwaites arrived to take over command of the Muscat Regiment, one of the three infantry battalions of the Sultan's Armed Forces. Peter was a serving British Army officer, commissioned into the Grenadiers, and he must have wondered what had hit him as he was welcomed by his Staff on a dusty airstrip surrounded by dark volcanic hills and a Beau Geste Fort shimmering in the near distance.

Equally his officers wondered what had persuaded this officer of distinction to swap the splendour of life in Windsor, Chelsea or Knightsbridge for service in the somewhat spartan conditions of one of the most isolated countries in the world.

The normal rotation of seconded commanding officers usually produced an infantryman and we were anxious to discover the hidden or certainly not obvious reasons for his volunteering for such a position.

All we knew was that here was a Gentleman of the Corinthian mould associated with Foot Guards Field Officers — a playwright, polo player and friend of the Royals. Few of us, on first impression, imagined he would become something of a legend in his own lifetime.

He was charming, witty and, judging by his slightly disapproving look, certainly rather shocked by the somewhat motley and renegade dress of his officers.

We learned on the first evening that he intended to improve all of our appearances and that his motto would be: 'Work Hard — Play Hard'.

The Sultanate of Muscat and Oman occupies the south-eastern corner of the Arabian Peninsula, flanked to the south by the seas of the Indian Ocean, to the west by the Great Arabian Desert and to the east by the Gulf of Oman. A country the size of Great Britain with a population of under one million, its only income was from the export of some vegetables, fish, dates and incense — most of which was shipped to Dubai for onward trade within the Gulf area. Oil was discovered in 1957 in commercial quantity and export of this vital resource began in 1967.

The strategic importance of Oman had been apparent since the earliest days of oceanic exploration. British involvement started in the early sixteen hundreds when the British East India Company established trading links and vied with the Portuguese, the Dutch and the French to gain prime position. The first Treaty of Friendship was signed in 1798, the main function of which was to exclude the French from Omani waters.

As ties were strengthened by frequently renewed and improved treaties between Oman and Britain, military aid was provided as and when a little local difficulty threatened the rule of the Sultan.

The 1951 Treaty established Oman as a major area of influence for the British Government and landing facilities were made available at the two permanent staging posts, RAF Salalah and RAF Masirah — Masirah being a small island off the Southern coast of Oman.

Since 1921 Britain had provided assistance to the Sultanate in recruiting, training and commanding the Sultanate Forces. These troops were mainly based in the north and used to quell localized wars between rival tribes and the not infrequent power struggles with the Iman.

In 1957 the Sultanate Forces were routed by the Iman Ghalib bin Ali al Hinai, with the at least tacit support of Saudi Arabia, who had a bilateral dispute with Oman over the ownership of the Buraimi Oasis. The Sultan requested aid from Britain and British Forces, mainly the Cameronians and two squadrons of the SAS, assisted the Sultan's Armed Forces.

The rebels had established a stronghold in the Hajar mountain range, the Jebel Akhdar (The Green Mountain) which dominates Northern Oman. It was a natural fortress rising steeply up to ten thousand feet with few routes which were easily defended. The rebels were finally routed by the combined force after a night ascent by the SAS.

This support and success further cemented the relationship and more military support was given to the Sultanate. The Sultan's Armed Forces were reorganized and regular British Army officers were seconded to SAF to help with training and Command. The officer corps was strengthened by the recruitment of contract officers. Seconded officers were normally only allowed to serve in Oman for eighteen months and, to provide continuity and bolster the numbers, contract officers — whose prime loyalty was to the Sultan — were attracted to this romantic, isolated and somewhat backward country. They were normally retired British Army officers and of varied background and experience. Some had passed their British Army 'sell-by' date, others had just become bored with endless tours of duty in BAOR. All added a certain air of mystery to SAF. Why were we all there? We were shortly to find out.

The background to the Dhofar Rebellion is covered in Chapter Two of Peter Thwaites' narrative. It became the Dhofar War because the Sultanate was just as strategically important as had been foreseen in the early sixteen hundreds. In the British Government's rush to divest itself of its overseas responsibilities and/or former centres of influence, the Wilson Government decided to leave the Aden Protectorate.

Oman commanded the Western entrance to the Persian Gulf through which fifty-six percent of the EEC, thirty percent of the US and ninety percent of the Japanese oil was shipped. The Wilson decision was a mistake that the Communist powers simply could not resist exploiting. After all, they had backed the Aden Nationalists and it was simply too mouth-watering to resist the temptation to back the Dhofaris and then continue a domino action through the feudal states of the Gulf, the Trucial Oman States and up to the prize of Kuwait.

The only barrier was the Sultan's Armed Forces. It would be a clandestine war as, due to British involvement, the Government had placed a D Notice on all reports. Reporters were banned from the country by the Sultan and — at the time Aden was handed over — there were anyway only eighteen serving British Army Officers at risk.

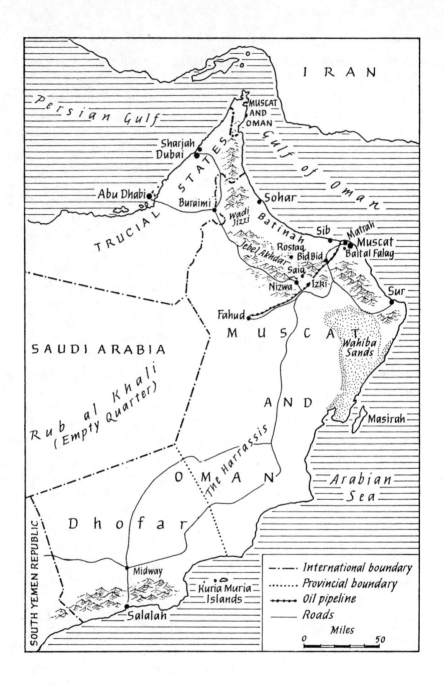

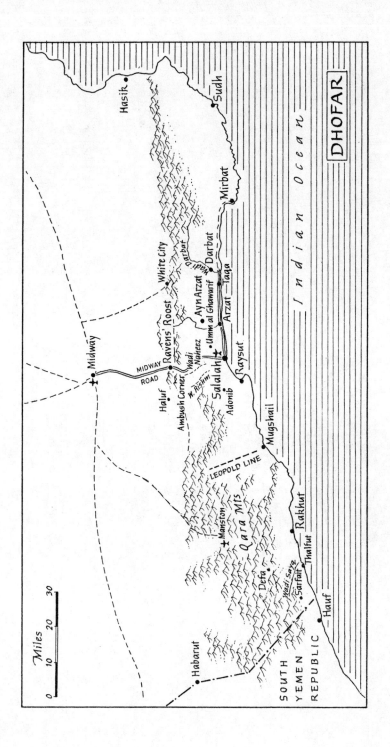

DHOFAR

1

The chain on the Vickers machine gun tapped gently against the tripod, uncomfortably loud to me but apparently unheard by the man carrying it on his back a yard ahead.

The whole battalion was strung out in single file on the one narrow goat track which let up the escarpment from the plain below. The rebels were somewhere on top. Half a moon shone palely on our feverish stealth and I thought of the casualties we would receive if there was a night ambush. In the past eleven months of the battalion's tour in Dhofar they had lost ten killed and twenty-two wounded, the rebels choosing just such vulnerable moments to attack, before picquets were out or the route cleared. They had not, however, hitherto operated much by night.

Bob Brown, the Desert Intelligence Officer, had received promising information that a group of about forty rebels of the Dhofar Liberation Front were living somewhere in the Jebel Harr, some fifteen miles west of Salalah, in an area two thousand feet up and accessible only by two well-defined tracks. They commanded observation over the plain for every inch of the route from Salalah over which we must travel. Thus we had motored at five miles an hour, without lights, and debussed some six miles from the forming-up place for the final climb. (Two years and many battles later I was to realize how futile these measures were, but now I was new and commanding my first major operation in the Dhofar province of Muscat and Oman.)

The track was narrow and stony and, though we wore rubber-soled boots or shoes, every stone displaced seemed like a thunderclap. We were early. I didn't want to take up our final positions until the first glimmer of dawn, so we halted, put out sentries and lay down in the dark to wait. No talking; no smoking. If a man went to sleep in the dark he got left behind. The sweat dried on our backs and it was suddenly cold. The escarpment was thick with small trees, camel thorn and rough foliage at this point. The men melted into the cover like shadows and lay silently, endlessly patient. One or two coughed. Officers and NCOs hissed at them to be silent but it is uncontrollable. Generations of malnutrition have induced a high rate of tuberculosis in the Arab soldier.

I lay on my back in the cradle of boulders and gazed at the blue-black sky, ablaze with stars, the Milky Way a bold white scar. I looked at my watch: 0330. The moon rose higher and brighter, but now we were in the shadow and needn't move until dawn. The rebels were late risers and I hoped we would be in a position to cut them off by first light. I thought over the plan again. It was strikingly simple in essence but might prove difficult to execute.

The enemy were reported to be living in various villages (nothing more than odd clusters of mud huts) near the top of the Harr escarpment. They tended to spend the nights there with their women and disperse into nearby caves by day. Hence our night approach: I hoped to catch them moving out at dawn. The chances of doing this were increased by approaching them from as many different directions as possible. To this end, Peter Raven's C Company had moved further east along the floor of the plain, climbed the escarpment by a different route and divided into two. Half would remain in concealed stop positions on the most likely escape routes and half, under Tony Carey, would move in a wide arc round to the north-east and link up with A Company which was leading my column in from the west. We should thus converge on the rebels from three sides. Even so, unless we caught them by surprise at close range in the early stages I was afraid they would go to ground, like old grouse, and stay in the copious cover until we had gone. I therefore planned to leave behind small ambush parties with long-hitting Vickers machine guns in well-concealed positions. Meanwhile, I would make a great show of withdrawing the whole force. There was nothing daringly original about this but it had worked well against the Communist terrorists in Malaya and elsewhere where small parties of guerrillas had proved reluctant to show their hand against a superior force.

0430. The air was chill and limbs stiffening. Richard John, commanding A Company lay a few yards away, his *shemag* wrapped around his head and face like an old woman. (A devoted Arabist, Richard: tall, languid, Major, Royal Scots Greys, far from his regiment's milieu of tanks and NATO and the plains of Saxony.) His Company would lead the next phase. Soon it would begin to get light. I wanted to be poised, ready to sprint across the open ground on top of the escarpment by the first glimmer of dawn. Peter Southwood-Hayton, the acting Adjutant, had made a reconnaissance of the route on an operation we had done a few weeks earlier and was now ready to guide us past the first group of *baits*[1]* that might harbour rebels. I moved to the front of the column with Peter where I could exercise control if we bumped anything and the soldiers rose silently to their feet, each man tapping the shoulder of the man in front, to keep the column closed up. The group of *baits* was close by the track (canalised at this point by precipitous rocks) where the ground opened out onto a plateau and I was afraid that the livestock would give warning of our approach. It was light enough to run now and we doubled past the mud and grass huts with nothing but the occasional dawn belch of the cattle to herald our coming. It was essential to get the cordon quickly into position to the north and west of the enemy area: C Company's stop positions should take care of the south and east. I signalled Mike Peele, second in command of A Company, to lead on past me and close the gap. They scampered by in their rubber-soled shoes, the gurgling of their water bottles the only sound.

I left an interval of some five hundred yards and then left with my tactical headquarters (Adjutant, three signallers, my orderly and a small escort). B Company fell in five hundred yards behind us. They were to provide one of the vital stay-behind parties with a Vickers machine gun and I left Derek Whittle (ex Sherwood Foresters and SAS) to choose a good place. The country was so open that I was afraid the enemy would spot us and stay well out of range of the rifle and light machine-gun fire (effective range three hundred yards). The Vickers, with its range of three thousand odd yards would help to correct this. 0530: Peter Raven breaks wireless silence to report his C Company stops in position on the south-

*See notes on p 171.

east slopes of the Jebel Harr feature and Tony Carey starting his move round to the north-east. Minutes later Derek Whittle (B Company) reports that his Company is in position behind me, the Vickers detachment with Nick Roberts already in the concealed positions it will occupy until tomorrow morning after the main body has withdrawn.

The stage was set. The overture was to be played by the Sultan's Air Force. The plan was that two armed Provosts would strike likely enemy positions within our cordon, in order to create movement. I hoped this would be the first evidence that the enemy would have of Security Forces anywhere in the area, would think it an air attack only (preparations for the operation had included numerous haphazard nuisance raids, unsupported by ground troops) and would come out of hiding to watch.

0600. Dead on time the two Provosts and a Beaver observation-communications platform were overhead. Jules Brett, the flight commander, circled once to give warning to the ground troops that he was coming in. (I prayed quickly that our map reading was good and we were all clear of the target area.) I looked up to see the tiny Provost apparently hanging by its tail in the cloudless sky. Then it dropped, like a silver minnow, and I heard Jules' laconic voice over the wireless: "Going in now". (How could he talk in that position?) Half a dozen fragmentation bombs burst in the tree-covered slopes round our objective, the sound muffled by the cavernous walls of the wadi. The second Provost came in with machine guns spitting from both wings. Even at that range it was a formidable sound and we were close enough to appreciate the morale effect of being in the target area. Two more impressive dives and Jules' voice sought permission to go back to base, re-arm, re-fuel and return to the fray.

John Cooper, my second-in-command, is up there in the escorting Beaver, acting as communications relay station. My half companies are so spread out and screened from each other by terrain that I could not otherwise have exercised control over all the out-stations, which included the artillery gun position on the plain and all the aircraft. The Beaver wheels lazily about the sky looking for enemy movement. The air strikes have failed signally to produce the disorderly enemy exodus I had hoped for. Anti-climax. The sun rises higher in the sky, smiling benignly on the wide, rolling upland and the long, bright green grass recently freshened by monsoon rain. The ground of this huge plateau is gently undulating, interspersed with trees and scrub and sudden rocky outcrops, all more reminiscent of Yorkshire or Devon than Arabia.

The Companies are fairly well concealed and I decide to wait a little longer before ordering the sweep. I would love a cigarette and a drink (tension dries the mouth as well as arid heat) but we have a long way to go. Anyway, these tribesmen can smell cigarette smoke a mile away (they say). Lance Corporal Dad Karim, my orderly, sits quietly dozing in the sun, festooned with extra water bottles and a haversack he refused to let me carry. He surfaces with a start as the sound of light automatic fire rips the air not far to our left. A Company has spotted something.

I grab the headphones of the wireless. Mike Peele's voice, then Peter Raven's. The firing continues from two directions. I resist the temptation to ask what's going on. Nothing more annoying for someone trying to fight a battle than a senior officer screaming for information. It becomes clear anyway. A and C Companies have the same sighting; two or three uniformed rebels moving on the tree-lined slopes somewhere beneath them. Like many incidents in this long day it fades into nothing. I tell them to sit tight. I don't like platoons and sections chasing shadows in different directions; loss of control, loss of the dominating positions we have achieved. Let the enemy move — and blunder into our stops.

0745. Tony Carey, with the other half of C Company moving into a group of houses eight hundred yards away. They will have buried their arms and uniforms well away from the village and now be playing the innocent herdsmen, scratching a living from the unforgiving cow. Tony starts a search.

Nothing seems to be happening on my immediate front, with A Company, nor in B Company's area some two thousand yards to the west. The ground rolls away to the south; thick grass, scented jasmine, butterflies, peace and beauty. According to my information there should be a group of *baits* about six hundred yards to our front, near the top of the escarpment, in which lives Mansoor, leader of this Eastern group of rebels.

I order Richard John's A Company to search and sweep and they move forward, one platoon covering the other. Peter Southwood-

Hayton, an old A Company man but temporarily acting as my battle Adjutant, begs to go with them. Richard could do with the extra officer and I say yes — but regret it almost immediately as it means that I have to man both the battalion command and air control wireless nets. A bad decision, but it soon becomes evident that Peter is worth his weight in gold with the search parties. His Arabic is excellent and it is a cruel, nauseating task. The huts are dank and airless with goats and calves mixed up with stale food, sour milk and pathetic, fly-blown children.

I move my Tac Headquarters to a small ridge overlooking the village and watch the soldiers moving from hut to hut, turning out the occupants. (Like clowns getting out of a baby car at the circus, fifteen people emerge from one round hut fourteen feet across.)

There is much wailing and howling and I feel like Herod.

Tony Carey's voice comes over the wireless, talking to John Cooper in the Beaver. He has seen a group of rebels moving rapidly away from the village he is searching. They are out of his range and he asks for the Provosts to make a low pass over them.

John's voice:

"Roger. Where are they?"

"Near the reservoir. Eight hundred — ten o'clock from my Tango[2]."

"Wilco. Out."

John relays the directions to the aircraft and minutes later I see the Provost diving low to the north. Comes the sound of light automatic fire, but it is not the swift ripple of the aircraft's machine guns. The rebels must be shooting at the Provost with an LMG. The plane flies out of my sight, then back again in a high, wide turn. Dives again. This time I hear the unmistakable sound of wing guns firing. A long pause, then Jules' tired voice:

"I seem to be on fire."

The transmission was intermittent and then cut out. I feared the worst. Jules in fact was preparing to bale out when the fire in his port wing was extinguished by his steep dive. In some pique he turned his plane into one last attack and emptied his guns into the rebel position before flying home. His starboard wing tank was empty and his port wing tank badly holed. He flew the aircraft at twenty degrees out of the horizontal to save petrol and landed safely.

Surely now we should be able to pin down the rebels who shot up Jules? I order Tony's half company and Derek Whittle's B Company about a mile to the west to link up and sweep the area.

Peter Southwood-Hayton comes on the air.

"Hallo — One. These *baits* are rotten with adoo[3] kit. Can we burn them?"

Must we? Should we? The homes of women and children. This is not total war.

"I'll come down and see you. Out."

I move the Headquarters a few hundred yards down the slope. There is a line of mud and grass huts built close under a small ridge. Soldiers quietly carry the few pathetic belongings out of the hut whilst the scattered groups of women and children squat on their haunches a few yards away. No men.

"Where are your men?"

"With the cattle and goats."

"Where?"

"Grazing — there —" a vague sweep of the arm.

"Which is Mansoor's house? We know Mansoor is the known leader of this group."

"We don't know. He doesn't live here any more."

Peter Southwood-Hayton comes up with a handful of .303 rounds and a khaki shirt.

"They're obviously adoo women, Colonel."

But are they? Every tribesman has a rifle by tradition; many are old Service .303s. Khaki shirts are worn by the rebels, certainly, but these are Dhofaris and there is a Dhofari squadron in the British-officered Trucial Oman Scouts some eight hundred miles to the north. Need they conclusively be rebels?

But now Richard comes up with two Adeni passports. I am new. Why shouldn't they have passports? No Dhofari has a passport legally. Anyone who leaves the country to find work elsewhere can only return as an illegal immigrant. The rebel base is at Hawf, in the East Aden Protectorate. Then a soldier comes up with two two-inch mortar bombs.

"I think we should burn the lot," says Peter. Richard John looks at me expectantly. An intensely human man, he loves Arabs.

"Give them ten minutes to get the livestock clear — and to talk, if they will. Then burn one in five." I turn away. Is this what I have come to Arabia to do?

A great wailing sound goes up when the women are told the verdict. Four houses in all burn like tinder and the wailing (rather too contrived, I think) rises to a crescendo, but nobody talks. I am told it will take them about eight hours to build another house.

The day drags on, sweeping and searching, marching, marching over that vastly deceptive area. B Company and half C draw blank on their search but find several pools of blood where the Provost attacked.

1730. It was time to start withdrawing. All the stay-behind parties had discreetly reconnoitred their ambush positions. Tony Carey, having marched his half company six miles in a gigantic half circle, linked up with A Company near the burnt houses. I was in touch with B Company some two miles to the north, but couldn't see them. Quite suddenly thick mist came down and after some futile directions on the wireless I borrowed Staff Sergeant Mohammed Isa and a small escort from A Company and went off to look for them.

"Stay where you are. I will come and guide you to the RV."

The rest of the battalion was now poised close by the only track down the escarpment and it might have been hours before B Company found us.

"Watch my Very light," I told Derek on the air. There was a chance they would see it through the low-lying mist.

"No good; watch mine." I heard the shot clearly, not far to the west.

Suddenly I saw three uniformed men moving on the skyline barely two hundred yards away. They moved well spaced out, quietly, cautiously. Must be B Company.

I waved and shouted. They stopped and waved back; a little uncertainly, then dropped to the ground, dissolving from sight. Mohammed Isa ran up the hill to try and contact them. I seized the wireless.

"Hallo Two — I have your right-hand sub-unit in sight. Tell them to stand up, stay where they are and I will close on them."

We stumbled up the hill in the mist. It would soon be dark and we must get down the escarpment. A night ambush on that track could lose us half a dozen men.

"Hallo Two," Derek's voice. "All my men are standing up. Over."

"They aren't. They've just gone to ground ahead of me. Get them to fire a Very light."

I heard a sharp report from the Very pistol — well to the south. Slowly it dawned on me that the three men must be rebels. We reached the top of the ridge and cast about, Mohammed Isa, Dad Karim, two signallers and the escort of five men. The whole might of my headquarters. No sign. The rebels had melted away. We had missed a great opportunity. (This was to be my first and only close sighting of live rebels in eighteen months of operations. I never saw the ones shooting at us.)

Ten minutes later we linked up with B Company in the mist. I hurriedly led them back to the rest of the battalion, still resting on the edge of the escarpment. We started the long walk home, covering each leg of the march with picquets on the prominent features. We passed through Peter Raven's C Company who were to stay out in ambush until the following day.

2330. All stay behind parties were in position for the long wait until dawn. The rest of the battalion returned to camp at Salalah. They were tired but in great spirits.

The final phase. In order to give the enemy the maximum time to run on to our ambush parties I decided not to withdraw these until midday, unless they were compromised. As soon as it was light the next day I gathered up the transport and the Reconnaissance Platoon to picquet the route and arrived at the foot of the escarpment; switched on to the battle command net. Peter Raven's voice talking to B Company.

"Hallo Two — close up to Callsign One and sweep towards me."

Good. He is ordering B Company to leave their ambush positions, link up with A Company's stay-behind parties and search the ground between them and his own C Company — the original stop line half-way down the escarpment.

There had been considerable activity in the early hours of the day. Soon after first light C Company had seen movement high on the ridge above their positions; suspected rebels but too far to engage. At 0650 Nick Roberts (B Company) sighted three rebels moving tactically across open ground eight hundred yards away, waited until they came nearer and opened fire with his Vickers. Missed the lot. Now the gaff was blown and they could expect no further rebel movement in that area. But at 0700 Mike Peele with A Company's ambush party saw other groups of rebels on the slopes between him and C Company to the south-east. Out of range, even for his Vickers, he held his fire and watched.

Peter Raven, the senior company commander, was in command of this phase of the operation. His company was the nearest to me (about three thousand feet above me but only a mile as the crow flies). I could thus hear his transmissions easily, but not those of A and B Companies deeper into The Jebel. There was a long pause while Nick Roberts collected his party and moved cautiously across open ground to link up with A Company and then C. Each party was very vulnerable on its own in open country, splitting into two halves, each covering the limited advance of the other. (The size of stay-behind parties is critical They must be small enough to conceal themselves in limited cover and yet large enough and with enough fire power to get themselves out of trouble when withdrawing.)

I was tempted to climb the hill again and command this last phase but decided against it. The numbers involved certainly didn't warrant my intervention and it would have appeared that I didn't trust Raven, who was a very experienced officer.

By midday B and A had linked up and the final sweep started. I was fairly confident that the rebels knew we had a number of scattered parties about and would stay out of trouble. They would not, however, miss a chance to hit us if they could do it without cost to themselves.

Almost immediately C Company's forward picquets were sniped at from about five hundred yards to the west. Good; there was a chance the culprits would be picked up by A or B as they closed in from that direction. It now seemed from the one-sided wireless transmissions I could hear that Peter Southwood-Hayton's party of A Company had a sighting. Raven was trying to establish whether these were the same lot as had been engaging his picquets or another party. They were certainly in the same general area.

Two Provosts had been flying discreet top cover[4] since first light and I now heard Raven calling for a strike. The first chill of foreboding struck me. It seemed clear that the rebels lay between Raven's C Company and Southwood-Hayton sweeping towards him from the west. Target indication would have to be faultless, since the pilot could not tell friend from foe from the air. Raven had clearly realized the danger since he started a long briefing to the pilot (Keith Wharton) and Southwood-Hayton.

Raven: "Three or Redcap 3 (the aircraft) My Tango — six hundred yards — two-four-0 degrees. Three adoo on north face of wadi. Over."

Wharton: "Roger — searching now."

Pause.

Raven: "Three for one (A Company). This must be near your location. Make sure you've got the panels[5] out."

I couldn't hear Southwood-Hayton's reply. There was another long pause.

Wharton: "I have them in sight. Three men running. Uniforms quite clear. Going in now."

The Provost climbed and turned and dived. As it pulled out of the dive I heard the ripple of its guns and Wharton reporting excitedly: "I think I've got one; Several fell."

Almost immediately Raven's voice: "Stop. Stop. They may be Call Sign One."

I still couldn't hear Southwood-Hayton but he must have said something. The sweat on me was suddenly cold. I asked for a sitrep and already feared the worst. At the very instant the Provos was diving Peter Southwood-Hayton's party had sighted a party of enemy five hundred yards away on the slope beneath them. Failing to hear Raven's instructions to the Provost and unaware that it was on its final run, Peter and one platoon had charged down the hill to close with the enemy. The Provost pilot assumed these were the rebels Raven was directing him on and attacked. Private Chaka, Peter's orderly, was shot through the wrist and Staff Sergeant Jan Mohammed received a burst through his right arm and leg.

The Provost was ordered to return to base and to send up a Beaver to airdrop stretchers to carry the wounded. They were also short of water. Raven reported that there was no hope of an aircraft landing on the slopes of the Jebel, so I set about making an airstrip on the coastal plain at the foot of the escarpment. Mercifully, this was flat and gravelly and only a few of the larger rocks had to be cleared. Drivers, operators, Gunners and the Recce Platoon set to. The strip was serviceable within an hour and I set off to meet the Companies coming down.

An hour later I meet them on the track. Chaka is young and frightened but can walk. Jan Mohammed, heavily doped with morphia, his right leg a mess, grins cheerfully and says he feels fine. An experienced, resourceful platoon commander, I can ill afford to lose him. (Could I have prevented it?) Eight men carry him gently down the precipitous goat track, those in front holding the stretcher shoulder high, those behind stooping low to keep him level. The bearers change every fifty yards. Everyone wants to carry him.

Slowly the rearguard files past me, all cheerful and smiling. I fall in behind, watching the covering party which will react to any enemy reaction as we withdraw. We reach the plain some two hours later, by which time Jules Brett has returned in the Beaver and is already making a low pass over the hastily-prepared strip. Thank God for Jules. He makes one quick pass and comes straight in, bounces high twice and applies his brakes to avoid overshooting into the sea. The wounded are ferried back to our Medical Post in Bahrain. Lawrie Lawrence, our superb Quartermaster, comes to meet us with huge containers of iced orange squash, enough for every man. The sun is high in the sky and we drink a quart each.

On the long drive back I reflect on the results of Operation "Final Fling". The returns were small for the effort involved. We heard later that only two rebels were confirmed wounded (one of whom died later), but at least we gained useful information about enemy areas and strengths and denied them the use for some time of one of their favourite bases for operations against the coast road. We had proved the efficacy of small ambush parties staying behind after the main body withdrew. (It was curious how this always seemed to work. Used a lot in the Malayan Emergency, I don't think it had been tried much in Dhofar before.) We had proved the need for a communications platform in the Beaver to keep wireless contact between widely dispersed sub-units (good) and had learned to our cost how easy it was for supporting aircraft to strike our own troops (bad). As we had seen, bad marksmanship could nullify the whole rigmarole of planning, administration and deployment if, at the one fleeting opportunity of a good target, (as with B Company's Vickers detachment) the man behind the gun failed.

"Final Fling" was the last operation before the Muscat Regiment went north to Oman for rest and retraining, after a year in Dhofar, but it was the first of its size to be carried out in the campaign against the Dhofar Liberation Front. After a series of company and patrol battles in which they had suffered occasionally heavy losses, the soldiers were reassured by the collective security of a battalion operation, well supported by guns and aircraft, and morale was high. On our next tour of duty, months later, we were to carry out many similar operations with some success.

When I got back to camp John Cooper told me that Jules Brett was discouraged to receive a signal from his Squadron Headquarters, six hundred miles away in Muscat, asking him to submit in writing why he had "hazarded his aircraft in low level attacks against the enemy". This news came to me whilst I was actually writing out a recommendation for Jules to be awarded a Sultan's Commendation for Gallantry throughout the operation. Luckily, he got his Commendation, rather than a reprimand. But the episode revealed for the first time a fundamental difference in approach towards the air support of ground troops between the Sultan's Air Force and the Army. It was to be emphasized again and again in the years to come, when the war in Dhofar increased in tempo far beyond the light-hearted overture of "Final Fling".

2

The kind, clever Colonel known as Piltdown Man had first suggested it. We were both working at the time for the Director of Military Operations at the Ministry of Defence — he as Colonel, General Staff, Military (MO) 4 and I as a General Staff Officer, Grade 2 in MO 1. The Directorate consisted of a Major-General (General Victor Fitzgeorge-Balfour), a Brigadier, General Staff and four branches each under a full Colonel, or Lieutenant-Colonel: MO 2, responsible for operational policy in the Far East (including Borneo, Singapore, Malaysia and Hong Kong); MO 3, which looked after Europe, NATO and (oddly) the Caribbean area; MO 4 the Middle East, and MO 1 the co-ordinating branch for the whole Directorate, responsible for such heady matters as global strategy and the operational aspects of every new item of equipment from a guided missile to a jungle boot.

"What are you going to do next?" said Piltdown Man as we passed in the corridors of power.

"I'm looking for something to command," I said.

"Have you ever thought of SAF?"

The Sultan's Armed Forces. Lines from a half-forgotten briefing fell into place. Muscat and Oman; independent Sultanate on the south-east coast of the Arabian peninsula; friendly to Great Britain with whom she was bound by a Treaty of Friendship (sounds a bit thin to me) since 1872; arid climate cooled by south-east monsoon; oil discovered in commercial quantities about 1965; Armed Forces of approximately brigade strength with British regular and contract officers; small air force with seconded and contract RAF pilots; active operations against a typical "Liberation Front" presently being conducted.

It seemed an interesting proposition after the long grind of Whitehall. For nearly two years I had sat in a large office with three other Majors and a Lieutenant-Colonel, reading papers and writing briefs for the DMO, Vice-Chief and Chief of the General Staff. It was the period of the Socialist Government's first Defence Review (followed with indecent haste by the second and third Defence reviews). The whole size and shape of our Defence effort was being rigorously examined and, inevitably, reduced, with the aim, not of making it more effective, but of keeping the Defence budget within £2,000,000,000 a year at then current prices. The basic difficulty in such a review was that the Government would give no clear direction on what they wanted to be able to achieve within that budget. They would not state clearly the reductions acceptable (say) in our contribution to NATO, in our Forces in the Middle and Far East; they would not specify the reinforcement capability required for a nuclear war in Europe nor the sort of intervention capability they required in a counter-insurgency or 'brushfire' war in a Commonwealth or Allied country. In short, they would not define their Defence policy. They would only, in effect, say, "See what you can do for £2,000M".

Thus, a number of studies were undertaken and papers written offering widely differing options under widely differing circumstances (or parameters as they came to be called, the right jargon had to be early acquired): a contribution to NATO as at present, plus a reduced presence in the Far East and nothing in the Middle East; a reduced contribution to NATO, a larger presence in the Middle East, a strategic reserve of one Brigade Group and nothing in the Far East; total withdrawal from both Middle and Far East but a battalion in each of Malta and Gibraltar and a Company in British Honduras? The options were wide-ranging, often bizarre, cost-saving in terms of men and money and invariably included, for reasons I was never at that time to discover, a sergeant and thirteen men of the Royal Marines in the Falkland Islands.

Papers flowed into MO like confetti and briefs were written for the Chiefs of Staffs Committee, the Defence Overseas Policy (a Cabinet) Committee and numerous other bodies which, between them, met every day of the week. The greatest burden fell on Steve Goodall, the immensely able GSO 1 of MO 1, but most of the papers had implications for all of us. Numbers and types of units

— Brian Kenny; the military aspects of ships and aircraft — Jack Fletcher (if carriers were scrapped how many more aircraft were needed, where would they be based and would this mean another military garrison?); weapons and ammunition of every sort — Jack Westlake; communications, chemical warfare, anti-aircraft, guided missiles, radar and anything electronic — myself, (who couldn't mend a fuse).

It was the time of drastic reduction in all development programmes. The revolutionary swing-wing bomber, TSR 2, was scrapped; aircraft carriers were to waste out and not be replaced; helicopter and weapons programmes were discontinued; the development of radar and communications systems, in which Britain led the world, was cancelled or curtailed; the Black Arrow rocket project cancelled; missile and surveillance systems scrapped or severely reduced in scope.

Each of the three Services and every branch of each Service fought furiously for its own development programme or equipment and the arguments adduced were expert, subtle, persuasive and ruthlessly partisan. They were also rather complicated. Papers on technological development were, inevitably, written by technological experts and the ability of these to write clear English was sometimes limited. They described in loving and incomprehensible detail the technical characteristics of their equipments but were often unable, even when cross-examined, to tell you of their practical application. It fell very heavily on the briefing staffs of the Chiefs of Staff to sift the practical wheat from the technological chaff and to recommend priorities among the many conflicting claims on the limited Defence budget. There was a great deal of departmental lobbying and the task of writing clear, balanced and objective advice, often at short notice, was sometimes a great strain.

My two years at Whitehall had been of unfailing interest, frequent frustration and considerable mental fatigue, in a position of influence, if not power, in the main policy-making branch of the Army Department. It was time to get back to soldiers.

In due course I received a communication from the Military Secretary's branch informing me that I had been "selected to command" the Muscat Regiment of the Sultan's Armed Forces (SAF). This delicacy of phrasing always amused me, implying as it did a long and painstaking quest by steely-eyed military researchers to find the right man for the job. The resulting promulgation sounded all right when the appointment was suitably impressive, but my sympathy lay with the ambitious soldier who was informed ceremoniously that he had been "selected" to command, say, a Base Workshops or a Mobile Laundry and Bath Unit. The processes of such selection were, to say the least, intriguing.

One of the advantages of being in Military Operations was that we saw all the Intelligence and Operational summaries relating to British military activities throughout the world, as well as many of the diplomatic telegrams. At this time the Indonesian confrontation was at its zenith, with a force of some 17,000 Commonwealth troops actively engaged in the Borneo jungle; the opposing political factions in Aden and its Protectorate had mobilized their thugs and were increasing the tempo of their attacks on British Security Forces, whose withdrawal had already been promised. There were occasional violations of the UN-controlled boundaries in Cyprus and occasional riots in Hong Kong. It was fascinating to read of the latest exploits of British forces world-wide before setting down to the serious business of the day — perhaps a brief on a paper discussing "The Application of Chemical Weapons to a European War in which the Nuclear Exchange has already taken place". (In short, what happens if you are gassed when you have already been fatally irradiated?)

Since my appointment to command a battalion in Muscat, I began to notice the inclusion in these intelligence reports of an increasing number of incidents involving the Sultan's Armed Forces on operations in Dhofar.

"SAF. A company of SAF on operations in Dhofar was ambushed by DLF at a water hole. Casualties: SAF — 3 killed; 8 wounded; DLF — not known."

It seemed a most unsatisfactory tally and the enemy always seemed to come off best. Sitting in a chair in Whitehall, it was easy to nod complacently and ask incredulously how an ambush could succeed in flat desert or why picquets weren't posted to guard against such activity. I was soon to know the answers. In due course, as each report of recent slaughter reached me I simply wrote "ouch" in the margin and passed it on to my colleagues.

The man from MO 4 (Middle East), who wore a perpetually

harassed expression at this time, loomed suddenly in front of my desk one day and announced the arrival on leave from Muscat of Captain Bob Brown, the Cameronians, the Sultan's Intelligence Officer for the Dhofar province of Muscat and Oman.

"He'll fill you in on the background," said MO 4 and departed. Almost immediately a dour, black-haired, nutbrown Scot appeared in my office and after considerable encouragement and a glass of rather nasty sherry I kept for special visitors, began to talk slowly, almost reluctantly, about Muscat.

The present trouble in Dhofar, it seemed, had its origins in a tribal conflict some seventy years ago, in which the then Sultan, the present ruler's grandfather, had been asked to arbitrate. Moving his court and a number of armed retainers six hundred miles across the desert from Muscat to Salalah, the Sultan made his decision, which was accepted by both sides. He would then have departed, but during his sojourn in this far flung corner of his domain he became most forcibly impressed by the very dramatic difference in climate between Muscat and Salalah. Muscat was cramped and stuffy, enclosed by black, volcanic, suffocating rock, in which no breeze stirred; Salalah was a sort of paradise, its coconut palms waving lazily in the soft winds of the Indian Ocean, its gardens watered by clear mountain streams and its fertile plain enriched for three months of the year by the south-east monsoon. Like God, the Sultan saw that it was good and decided to stay. He built a large, rambling grey stone palace on the sea shore and thereafter divided his time between the seat of government in Muscat and his country seat in Dhofar. This was not what the recalcitrant tribes had bargained for. Notwithstanding the fact that they had asked him to intervene in the first place, they had traditionally regarded the inhabitants of Muscat and Oman as foreigners and abhorred the thought of this alien ruler residing with them for all time. Ethnically, there was some justification for their antipathy. The tribes of Dhofar are not true Arabs and are thought to have originated from the Yemen or even Ethiopia. They have their own peculiar glottal language and customs which are totally different from the rest of the Sultanate.

Time passed and, never quick to forget a grudge, the Dhofaris managed to nurse this one for the next seventy years.

Meanwhile the oil prospecting companies had come to Dhofar and were carrying out their esoteric procedures in the desert due north of Salalah's surrounding mountains. So too had come His Highness Sultan Said bin Taimur, 16th Abu Saidi ruler of Muscat and Oman, not just to visit Salalah to rest from the cares of state, but to live permanently in his palace there. Change and discovery were abroad throughout the whole of Arabia; some said the streets of Jedda were paved with gold; the people of Kuwait and Abu Dhabi were given free houses, medicines, hospital treatment and learning for their children, so great was the new-found wealth beneath their sands. In nearby Aden and the Hadhraumaut there was, unfortunately, no oil, but by God, if the British were going there would be political and material spoils for all. Change and decay, unrest and revolt were in the air.

The disease spread to Dhofar, where it crystallized in the scrofulous person of one Salim bin Nufl, sometime Sultanic driver, sacked for inefficiency and bearing a king-sized grudge. Oil had been discovered in the desert, south of Muscat, and although not a penny in royalties was yet forthcoming, it was easy to generate ill-wind against the Sultan's autocratic rule, his failure to provide social services for his people, his rigid application of Koranic law and his absolute dependence on British advisers in both the Government and Armed Forces of his country.

In 1964, gathering together forty odd similarly rebellious subjects, Salim bin Nufl fled to Saudi Arabia to enlist aid for a proper uprising. King Faisal, whose antagonism towards the Sultan stemmed from a long-standing dispute over ownership of the Buraimi Oasis, was not averse to granting the rebels aid and guerrilla training and the supply of arms and vehicles to foster rebellion.

Duly primed, bin Nufl and his forty followers crossed the Rub al'Khali (the Empty Quarter between Saudi Arabia and Dhofar) in seven Dodge power wagons and established themselves in the mountains north of Salalah. From here they successfully ambushed the oil company's vehicles traversing the Midway Road and, when elements of the Sultan's army followed up this outrage, they ambushed them too, with equal success. Luckily, however, some hawk-eyed pilot of the Sultan's Air Force spotted the Dodge power wagons, which were then destroyed by an air strike and a soldier of the Muscat Regiment, reaching for a stone after the morning's bowel movement, uncovered the first buried rifle of the rebels' main arms cache. This set the self-styled Dhofar Liberation Movement back a bit and the initiative was further maintained by two nicely judged cordon and search operations, one by the Muscat Regiment which picked up some ninety unsuspecting Salalah townsmen actively sympathetic to the rebels' cause and the other by the First Battalion Irish Guards, who sailed from Aden into the rebels' main support base at Hawf, just over the Dhofar border in South Yemen, and arrested some fifty wanted men. All these potential insurrectionists were screened and interrogated by Bob Brown and eventually ordered to be detained at the Sultan's pleasure. The Sultan was a merciful man. In obedience to Koranic law, he never took the lives of his prisoners. High on the parched black rock surrounding Muscat harbour was a terrible fort called Jelali, built by the Portuguese in 1589. Here languished the Sultan's enemies, heavily shackled with great iron bars between their ankles; smugglers, murderers, political agitators, adulterers, debtors — and rebels.

The situation, Bob Brown told me in his sepulchral Scottish tones, was now reasonably stable. A battalion of SAF was deployed in company bases on the Jebel above Salalah and provided escorts for the oil company convoys along the Midway Road and patrolled actively in search of the rebel forces. The rebels treated SAF with a certain respect, lay in wait, endlessly patient, and would unfailingly ambush them if they could do so without loss to themselves. They appeared to be husbanding their resources until the British forces withdrew from Aden, after which they could expect to receive greater support from the emergent state, whichever political faction assumed control.

Bob Brown was a most gifted Intelligence Officer. His ability to marshal a mass of conflicting information, to evaluate, discount and discard, and his interpretation of what remained, was masterly. But the campaign in Dhofar finally defeated him, as it defeated many Intelligence Officers. His task required him to glean information from any source which offered it, regardless of race, creed or station. In this, inevitably, he had to deal with factions or individuals sometimes unsympathetic, sometimes hostile, more often supremely indifferent to His Highness Said bin Taimur. The Sultan considered that Captain Brown, ostensibly in the pursuit of Intelligence, was associating with undesirable elements of the population and interfering with affairs which were not his province. This could not be permitted. In his quest for the information on which the Security Forces depended for their success, as I was soon to discover, Bob Brown was as surely shackled as the Sultan's prisoners in Jelali jail.

3

The RAF VC 10 circled over the mass of grey, volcanic rock and finally landed on the glaring concrete runway of Khormaksar. Wire and sandbagged emplacements surrounded the RAF station and there was an air of quiet watchfulness reminiscent of Egypt 1954, Cyprus '58, British Guiana '65 and all those other areas of nationalist crisis and British involvement that I had witnessed. For this was Aden in 1967, in the death throes of an orderly British withdrawal. Hither I had been sent, fresh from the corridors of power, to learn Arabic, so that I might communicate with the soldiers I was to command.

I was met by a charming, purple-faced Irishman with a double-barrelled name which escapes me, who introduced himself as a Major, retired, administrative officer of the Middle East School of Arabic. He wore an eyeglass, which in the prevailing humidity was usually steamed up, and a large moustache, the droop of which, I was to discover, varied in accordance with his mood and sobriety. When he was drunk or depressed it sagged visibly, but there were moments in the late forenoon when its tilt was quite jaunty. It was now in the very early hours of a Sunday morning and it was hanging untidily over his lower lip.

During the long evening vigil, while waiting to meet my flight, the Major had clearly not been idle.

He conducted me through the cluster of RAF Security and Movements staff, Customs and Immigration officials with a vaguely proprietorial air and out to a small bus, in which we drove the short distance to Seedaseer Lines. Every yard of the route was flanked with barbed wire and lit by the bright perimeter lights of numerous encampments. The Major hiccoughed gently, pointed out landmarks which seemed notoriously insignificant in that flat waste land and finally deposited me in a small, air conditioned bedroom near the Officers' Mess and bade me a cheery good morning.

My head had hardly touched the pillow when the opening bars of Beethoven's Fifth Symphony, amplified to about 115 decibels and apparently booming from three stereophonic speakers, jolted me fully awake. I endured this cacophony for some twenty minutes, for it seemed churlish to make a fuss so soon after arrival in a new Mess, but eventually I could stand it no longer, stumbled into the bright Arabian night and quickly traced the noise to a room some thirty yards away. Here I beheld the Irish Major reclining in a chair, his eyes closed, moustache hanging in a limp grey fringe, conducting the unseen orchestra with a half empty glass of whisky. This was clearly no prelude to my introduction to Arabic and I politely asked him if he would mind turning the volume down a little. There was no response. It seemed a pity to wake him, so I crossed the room, tentatively reduced the machine's volume, gauged his reaction, which was negligible, and finally silenced it altogether. The Major's glass hand was still waving gently as I left.

The situation in Aden in these last months of British rule was the tragic outcome of the policy of successive British governments, not to fail to formulate a strategic plan in the Middle East, but to stand firm on that plan when it was threatened. The policy, rightly or wrongly, was to maintain a military presence, or at least the capability to intervene militarily, in the Middle East.

To do this required a base — a huge complex of stores, vehicles, weapons and ammunition, together with the troops to protect it and the ports and airfields to support it. Thus a succession of military bases was established — the Canal Zone of Egypt, Cyprus, Kenya, Aden and, later and to a lesser extent, Bahrain. Each cost millions of pounds and each, as the pressure for decolonization from nationalist, terrorist and subversive elements increased, was surrendered. The lesson which took so long to be learned was that a base anywhere depends for its survival either on local goodwill or on the determination (and money) in the face of local opposition to maintain it by force. In Aden this lack of determination, this loss by Britain of the will to rule, was never more apparent.

The political aim, consistent throughout the post-war abandonment of Empire, was to get out, leaving, if possible, a situation of stable and responsible self-government, but at all costs to get out. In Aden and its Protectorate this self-government was to be achieved by the so-called Federation of South Arabia. Here was the fundamental false hope. Federations have rarely been successful; in South Arabia it was doomed from the start. It was hoped, apparently with genuine sincerity, that the eleven feudal states of the hinterland surrounding Aden would join happily — or at least viably — with the comparatively sophisticated urban population of Aden itself. The upcountry states were a mixture of totally feudal and primitive sultanates and sheikdoms, traditionally warring amongst each other and inhabiting great tracts of almost waterless and roadless mountains. In Aden, a polyglot society of Adenis, Yemenis, Egyptians, Indians, Pakistanis, Somalis, Jordanians and others were flexing their muscles for the big political struggle which would inevitably ensue. Egyptian-sponsored Arab nationalism, Russian and Chinese-sponsored Communism and militant left-wing trade unionism were the unhealthy factions which were contending with each other to dominate the scene; factions which needed firm measures by the British colonial administration to be kept in check.

The Adenis' main complaint, which had some justification, was that the up-country sheikhs were being given too big a share in the government of the new Federation. Armed terrorism — the inevitable concomitant of twentieth century political unrest — first showed itself in 1963, when a grenade was thrown at the then High Commissioner, Sir Kennedy Trevaskis, which missed him but fatally wounded Mr. George Henderson, who gallantly threw himself forward at the critical moment. This tragic and murderous incident marked the beginning of a rising tide of violence which continued until the last British troops left in November, 1967.

As had happened elsewhere, the British Government's announcement of ultimate withdrawal prompted the more irresponsible political factions to increase their programme of shooting, bombing and sabotage so that they could claim that their 'freedom fighters' were driving out the British.

The tragedy, of course, was that the people of Aden and its Protectorate were not particularly anti-British, any more than the people of Palestine, Malaya, Kenya, Cyprus or British Guiana had been. We did them no harm, we administered them well and they liked our money. Above all they respected strength and firmness of purpose, which the British administration, in the face of so-called "world opinion" so often denied them. Hatred, fear, distrust and revenge were deliberately fostered by the politically motivated minority.

The two main political organizations responsible for terrorism were the National Liberation Front (NLF) and the Front for the Liberation of Occupied South Yemen (FLOSY). Perhaps the whole vicious, puerile campaign was typified by the latter title. "Liberation" was unnecessary since the British Government had already volunteered to terminate the "Occupation" in any case, but the very word "liberation" implied a just and necessary struggle.

The struggle consisted firstly of assassinating the Special Branch officers of the Aden Police, on whom the Security Forces depended for their intelligence; secondly, intimidating the civilian Arab population and promoting civil disobedience, riots, strikes and unrest, and thirdly making opportunist attacks by rocket, grenade and small arms fire on the Security Forces and on any British Civilian who presented an easy target. The aims of both factions of terrorists were broadly similar. First, to discredit the newly-formed, politically rightish, Federal Government and frustrate progress towards a stable South Arabia. Second, thereby to create a vacuum which could later be filled by Egyptian and Russian influence. Third, to give the impression that the British were being "defeated" and driven out by superior "liberating" forces.

There were very simple and well-tried measures available to defeat these aims, but the necessary political support for them was not forthcoming. A true state of emergency should have been declared and drastic but necessary measures put in force, such as the evacuation of service families, the death penalty for carrying unauthorised weapons and strict enforcement of curfews. The situation is best summarized in Lieutenant-Colonel Colin Mitchell's admirable book *Having been a Soldier* when he quotes a letter written by a Royal Northumberland Fusiliers officer serving in Aden at the time; "There is now no deterrent to the terrorist. No terrorist has been executed although many have been caught red-handed. Captured terrorists are placed in Mansoura Detention Centre where the standard of living is a great deal higher than any of them enjoyed before being caught. The terrorists know they will be released as heroes in a year or eighteen months when we go. The only thing a terrorist is afraid of is being caught and shot by an alert soldier or sentry while carrying out his act of terrorism."

With the scales weighted so heavily against the maintenance of law and order, the tide of terrorism surged needlessly on. We had to go; but we could at least have gone with dignity.

"Sabah-al-Khair!"

"Sabar-an-Noor!"

"Khayf hal-kum?"

"Tamam, al hamdu l'illah."

Every day for the next three months students and teacher greet each other thus. Good morning (literally, we were told, "Morning of the good; morning of the light.") How are you? Well, thanks be to God. Never in my subsequent two and a half years in Arabia did I use these expressions again, for this was an urban, civilized greeting and in the primitive sands of Muscat and Oman the more religious *"Salaam alaikum." "Wa' alaikam as-Salaam"*[6] was used, muttered over and over again, like a litany.

There was a wide assortment of students on the final course of the Middle East Command School of Arabic; officers and senior NCOs destined for the British-sponsored Trucial Oman Scouts, the newly-formed Abu Dhabi Defence Force, the Sultan of Muscat's Army — but never his Air Force, which was a grave error. We were taught by a weird assortment of instructors. There were the most able officers of the Royal Army Education Corps who had been on the long Arabic Course at the Middle East College of Arabic Studies in Beirut — and spoke slow, meticulous, classical Arabic which was easy for another Englishman to understand but, repeated some months later to some rough, hairy Bedu, was received with polite incomprehension or open-mouthed astonishment. There was a large, black Palestinian Arab called Mr. Hussein and a small drunken Adeni Arab called Mr. Othman Rani and there was a spry, amusing Jordanian Arab called Mr. Shirvani. This brave man also ran a local newspaper in which he consistently warned his readers of the dangers of violence daily perpetrated by the NLF and FLOSY. "Beware that we do not exchange one form of slavery for another . . ." he thundered almost daily in his editorial, apologizing the following morning to his class for describing "the benevolent British rule as slavery". He was twice beaten up by FLOSY thugs during the long hot summer of 1967 and finally murdered after the British withdrawal.

Aden was the sixth area in which I had served while the British Government and administration were drawing to a close[7]. I was thus anxious to see as much of the action as possible — and the School of Arabic didn't seem likely to further this wish, apart from the occasional storm over Arabic irregular verbs.

Luckily I had friends in three of the battalions then doing duty in the Federation; 1st Battalion Irish Guards, 1st Battalion the Parachute Regiment and the Queen's Dragoon Guards. Each kindly agreed to show me round their operational areas.

The Micks were, as ever, full of regimental pride, good humour and hospitality. After numerous beautifully organized parties at their Mess at Little Aden I shamelessly asked Tony Aylmer, their commander, if I could visit their positions up country in the Radfan, at Habilayn and Dhala.

This was the cradle of the original campaign in 1964, when Yemeni-inspired dissident tribesmen had initiated the move to force the British Administration into a premature withdrawal. Here, some two brigade groups had been deployed, supported by considerable air power, and men of the 22nd Special Air Service Regiment (SAS) had fought hopeless last ditch battles and had the heads chopped from their lifeless bodies for their pains. Here too more recently, the Irish Guards had been in action for the first time since Palestine 1948 and won a Military Cross, a Military Medal and numerous other citations for gallantry.

Habilayn lay sixty miles north of Aden, on the main route to the Yemen. It was a high, wide plateau, ideally suited for development into a forward airfield, surrounded by smaller hills which provided for its immediate close defence, the whole surrounded at a distance of several miles by a heartless wilderness of mountainous volcanic rock, from which parties of well-armed tribesmen issued almost nightly to attack the camp with great skill. It was not unlike the campaigns of the North-West Frontier of India in the thirties. Luckily, the Arab idea of attack is usually confined to shooting off the maximum amount of ammunition at the opponent from behind a distant rock, without the nasty physical involvement of a hand-to-hand assault. This very sensible and civilized aversion in Arab soldiers was one of the main problems I was soon to try to overcome.

I travelled round the Micks' positions with Tony Aylmer in a Sioux helicopter, impressively riddled with bullets from a recent clash with the rebels and most expertly flown by Simon Gordon-Duff. Simon told me that the Army Air Corps pilots had been having a very exciting time marking rebel positions with red smoke dropped from their slow-moving, very vulnerable helicopters, before the RAF flew in to strike the target with their Hunters. The different attitudes of the RAF and Army Air Corps towards low level flying over enemy positions were already sharply defined.

The main position at Habilayn was held by battalion headquarters, two rifle companies and an assortment of supporting artillery and armoured cars. The effect was not unlike the defensive positions of the First World War, with deep communication trenches linking heavily sand-bagged dugouts and surrounded by barbed wire fencing. We spent a peaceful night, although the proving of weapons and defensive fire tasks made sleep difficult. This involved an almighty barrage of fire at about eleven o'clock, from machine guns, mortar and artillery on to the very areas from which you hoped the enemy would attack. I have always thought the practice counter-productive. First, it told the watching enemy exactly where your defensive fire was laid, secondly, it deterred his attack when you should really be inviting it on your own terms, and thirdly, it wasted ammunition.

Further north, a few miles from the Yemen border, the remaining rifle company held the ridge at Dhala. The Dhala valley was one of the most attractive and fertile areas in the whole Protectorate; mile upon mile of verdant crops, maize, vetch and qat, which the Arabs chew, grew under a delightful climate and plentiful rain. But the vulnerability of the camp horrified me. Sited on a long, narrow ridge, it protruded from the surrounding plain like an iceberg on a flat sea. On to this ridge were crammed tents, weapon pits, fire positions, ration and ammunition stores, officers' and sergeants' mess tents and a volleyball pitch. An incendiary bullet or phosphorus bomb would have cleared the ridge of canvas in a few minutes. This was not intended in any way as a criticism of the selective powers of the commanders responsible. I am sure they had no choice.

The local political situation contributed in some measure to the vulnerability of this company position. The Emir of Dhala, who lived in a glaring white palace nearby, extorted a toll from those passing through his domain. Since this was on the direct route into hostile Yemen it was a simple matter for dissident tribesmen quite legally to approach the very gates of the camp, still carrying their traditional weapons and lie up until dawn to snipe, mine or booby trap while passing through. There were two principal opponents, Ali Antar and Ali Aktar, whose dislike of the Emir and the British was exceeded only by their hatred of each other, so they never joined forces. However, the Micks received their share of attacks by both these and other dissident tribesmen and were lucky to escape comparatively unscathed.

The battalion's role in the Radfan was partly to protect the installations there but also to provide patrols designed to win the hearts and minds of the inhabitants of the less accessible regions. As Peter Verney says in his excellent book *The Micks,* "For these forays the helicopter was essential and liaison with the RAF and the Army Air Corps throughout the up-country tours was the most important feature of their activities. The helicopters were in constant use either for ferrying troops, or for supplying them in their forward positions, or for conveying commanders from one area to another. It was a new medium of war, but one they found absolutely essential in this inhospitable terrain; to command operations from the air or to establish aerial pictures to cover some approach march requires a speed of reaction far removed from the pedestrian thinking of normal infantry soldiering. It was a highly instructive experience for everyone."

In Dhofar, later that year, I tried to carry out the same tasks, including more or less continuous casualty evacuation — but without the helicopters.

Joe Starling, who had been a student at the Staff College with me in 1958, was now second in command of the Parachute Battalion and took me on a patrol to visit their positions in and around Sheikh Othman, a village three or four miles outside Aden which was one of the worst trouble spots at this unhappy time, and the scene of almost continual exchanges of fire. (Mr. Othman Rani lived there, and frequently arrived for work at the Language School with a visible hangover, having spent the night lying flat on the floor of his room surrounded by crates of beer supplied by sympathetic pupils.)

I arrived at the Officers' Mess to find the assembled officers eating generously-cut sandwiches and slabs of warm, damp fruitcake. After this we emerged to view an amazingly impressive escort of Landrovers drawn up outside the orderly room, each vehicle barely visible for its load of parachutists armed to the teeth, their combat smocks and equipment hung about with Sterling machine guns, grenades, wireless sets, binoculars, Very pistols and other impediments of war. At a word from Joe the small convoy took off at high speed for their forward Battalion Headquarters at Sheikh Othman. Speed and alertness were the antidotes for sudden ambush or random shots from the terrorist forces in the area. I was most impressed with the Parachutists' professionalism and battle drill, whereby everything was done at top speed and with the minimum orders from officers and NCOs.

We shot through Checkpoint Charlie, a huge sandbagged emplacement at the vortex of a flat, open crossroads, regularly shot up by terrorists, round "Grenade Corner", and finally arrived at Fort Walsh, formerly the Police Station at Sheikh Othman.

As we disembarked from the Landrovers, still at high speed, there was a nasty crump nearby which bespoke the favourite terrorist weapon of the time — a Blindicide rocket launcher. This was followed by several long bursts of light machine-gun fire from the other side of the high wall which separated the Fort from the main street. I never discovered at whom, or by whom, these shots were directed, but presumed the Blindicide at least was meant for us, as the whole tower of the Fort was protected by a wire mesh screen designed to detonate the rocket comparatively harmlessly about four feet from the walls. Judging by the holes in the masonry, the device was only partly effective.

The Parachute Battalion, most ably commanded by Mike Walsh[8], dominated their area by a system of strongly defended observation points, which drew regular bursts of terrorist fire from small arms, rocket and mortars, and were linked by foot patrols and supported by the armoured cars of the Queen's Dragoon Guards. This form of aggressive containment was fairly typical of British army tactical thought during most of the post-war counter-insurgency campaigns, and I was to question its efficacy more than once when I came to command a battalion in Muscat.

More often than not, it seemed to me, this pattern of "aggressive patrolling" was dictated by little more than a kind of military inferiority complex — a desire to demonstrate a superiority which didn't exist. It didn't exist because in none of these situations was the Army allowed to deploy that strength which would have given it superiority. Over the years, in Palestine, Egypt, Cyprus and now Aden, "aggressive patrolling" in an urban guerrilla environment had too often meant sending soldiers out on foot patrol, inadequately supported by fire (because the buildings from which that close support should have come were occupied by a hostile population) and with instructions to use only minimum force. This forbade them to open fire before the opposition, a restriction which from the outset denied them the initiative. They were like so many Aunt Sallies. The results were, to my mind, too many unnecessary casualties with no compensating military gain.

In any shooting war he who moves in sight of the enemy is at a disadvantage. The aim should be to sit tight and make the enemy move, concentrate and thus be easier to destroy. This is never more essential than in a guerrilla environment, but because it is a primarily defensive concept the British Army has appeared reluctant to adopt it. And yet Wellington's greatest victories resulted from choosing strong defensive positions and drawing the enemy repeatedly to attack them at a disadvantage. This I was to try on an infinitely smaller scale, but with limited success, in the following year.

Thanks to George Powell, another Staff College friend, I was also able to go out on an armoured car patrol of the Queen's Dragoon Guards which he commanded. These lumbering vehicles crept around the narrow streets of Sheikh Othman, their engines shattering the night air, totally at the mercy of terrorist rocket or mine attack. I have seldom felt so helpless or frightened. It was generally considered that Sheikh Othman was a good deal "hotter" than the more publicized Crater Area of Aden itself. However, from the end of June until the final withdrawal from the Protectorate it was Crater which became the talisman of all good newspapermen and stole the headlines; Crater and the Argylls — both expertly stage managed by Lieutenant-Colonel Colin Mitchell.

Students on the Arabic course were quartered in the very comfortable Officers' Mess of the Federal Regular Army (FRA), the Adeni national army still commanded by a British Brigadier and with a large number of British seconded and contract officers. Into the FRA Officers' Mess, at about tea time on 20 June, came a very hot and bothered British officer who said he had been barricaded into his own office for most of the day while two tribal factions of the National Guard, to which he was seconded, were shooting at each other. This was in Champion Lines, close to Khormaksar airfield and overlooking the polo ground. Once discipline had snapped the Arab soldiers went berserk, firing indiscriminately at both the airfield and at nearby Radfan Camp, which Mike Walsh's Parachute Battalion were sharing with the Lancashire Regiment.

The mutineers soon turned their attention towards a more ambitious target. A party of soldiers of the Royal Corps of Transport were returning from practice on the rifle range and these men were caught in their truck in the open, quite defenceless and mercilessly shot down. Eight were killed. Obviously the situation required firm handling and a company of the King's Own Border Regiment, attached to the Parachute Battalion, were dispatched to restore order.

Meanwhile, an exaggerated account of these confused events had reached Crater by word of mouth. "The British are shooting at Arabs of the National Guard." It must be remembered that this was only two weeks after the Six Day Arab-Israeli war. The Egyptians had been ridiculed before the eyes of the world and Arabs everywhere were feeling frustrated, humiliated and belligerent. Emotions were running high and nowhere were they more volatile than in Crater, the citadel of Aden and headquarters of the two main terrorist organizations, the NLF and FLOSY. In Crater, too, was the headquarters of the Aden Armed Police, who were known to have been penetrated by both the terrorist gangs. Hearing the garbled reports of Arab-British fighting outside Crater, the Armed Police announced from their barracks that they would shoot any British soldiers who approached the city.

At this time the 1st Battalion Royal Northumberland Fusiliers were responsible for the security of Crater and, approaching the end of their very successful tour of duty, were in the process of handing over the area to the advance party of the 1st Battalion the Argyll and Sutherland Highlanders. Each patrol of the outgoing Fusiliers was accompanied by representatives of the Argylls and thus it was, at about eleven o'clock on the morning of 20 June, that joint reconnaissance patrols into the hitherto comparatively peaceful district of Crater found a totally different and hostile situation. Hastily constructed road blocks had been thrown across the road, and men from the Armed Police barracks had taken up fire positions behind barricades and on top of buildings.

Even in the bizarre situation then obtaining in Aden, it seemed incredible that the Armed Police, who were part of the security forces in this still small British colony and jointly responsible with the British troops for the maintenance of peaceful law and order, should be acting in this blatantly hostile and irresponsible manner, but so it was. Into this ambush drove two Landrovers containing two company commanders and their escorts; the outgoing Fusilier company commander John Moncur, and the relieving company commander of the Argylls, Brian Malcolm, whom I had met in their Mess a few days before.

In the broad boulevard outside the Police barracks the ambush was sprung. The two officers, their drivers and wireless operators, were riddled with bullets from machine guns, light automatics and rifles, and the Landrovers burnt. Eight more British soldiers lay dead to add to the RCT massacre earlier in the day.

In this horrifying incident lay the seeds of the so-called Crater controversy, which received much publicity at the time. Crater was now clearly controlled by the terrorist organizations whose dupes were the Armed Police. Natonalist elements were jubilant, the Crater area was declared an independent republic by the extremists. No live British troops remained in the area and although an amnesty was arranged for four o'clock that afternoon to allow a British ambulance to collect survivors (there was only one), British troops were ordered to stay out of Crater until further orders.

This was regarded by most serving soldiers in Aden at the time as a humiliating defeat and a shameful appeasement. Colin Mitchell, whose battalion of Argylls assumed responsibility for the area a few days later, wanted to lead his battalion in a straightforward infantry assault on the town. This of course was rejected by Major-General Philip Tower's Middle East Command and the prevailing political advice because of the consequences of a pitched battle with the Arabs. It was argued that the re-entry of Crater would require a brigade attack supported by heavy weapons and would invite heavy casualties, both military and civilian, and extensive damage to property. The flames engendered might well spread to the rest of Aden and to the hinterland, where a mutiny of the tribally-divided Federal Regular Army would lead to a major battle. This would prevent the achievement of the overriding military and political aim of the time — a peaceful withdrawal of the British presence.

I had some sympathy with both points of view. As a soldier with some experience of recent political interventionism in military decisions, I loathed inaction and the insidious wait-and-see attitude now being counselled. I have always favoured firm decisive action in the earliest stages of a situation of unrest as the best means of preventing its escalation. However, at this stage of the Crater crisis I believed that it was already too late for precipitate military action on the grand scale. This should have come much earlier — in a firm military control of Crater from the outset. Now, I believed that Tower was right and Mitchell wrong. It was wise to wait and negotiate. This policy was vindicated three days later when, after many apologies for misunderstandings and considerable political negotiation, the Argylls entered Crater without a shot being fired.

It was yet one more example of the effect of political expediency on military decision — and no military operation in peacetime can be free of it. Often it is proved catastrophically wrong, the classic example being the political reluctance to allow immediate small-scale military intervention in the Canal Zone of Egypt in March, 1956, when Nasser revoked the Agreement, signed only two months before, whereby we could maintain our stockpiles of vehicles and equipment using civilian contractors. A battalion could have been flown in from Cyprus within hours and enforced our right to guard our national property. Instead, high level vacillation and inaction led to the ponderous, inexcusable and disastrous invasion of Port Said by French and British forces some six months later.

The politicians are often wrong, sometimes right. Sometimes they are in the position of knowing all the facts — seeing the bigger picture — of which the soldier will be ignorant. Sometimes the soldier, as the man on the ground, will know more from his immediate feel of the situation than the politicians can ever know. The irony of the Crater situation was that the Federal Government, which at that time our political masters were so anxious to support, collapsed a few months later and was overthrown by the NLF, even before the British withdrawal. Colin Mitchell wrote aggrievedly,[9] "Therefore the events of 20 June, 1967, in Crater were a classic example of military judgement being influenced by political expediency." But so it will always be.

4

The course continued; Arabic irregular verbs in the morning, homework in the afternoon, the evenings quiet. Terrorism had closed all restaurants and places of entertainment and the hot black nights were mostly spent in private houses or watching the kindly Irish Major conduct his unseen orchestra through varied programmes of symphony and opera. Sometimes, at the height of an orgiastic cadenza, he would fall off his stool and be carried quietly to bed by a sympathetic audience.

From September of the previous year, ever since I had been 'selected' to command the Muscat Regiment, I had been receiving letters from the present commanding officer, urging me to come out early and get to grips with the job, pages and pages of gratuitous information about the life and conditions of service in the SAF, personalities I would have to deal with, the operational situation, the character of the Sultan and so on. Those rose to a crescendo of literary output when I arrived in Aden, when it soon became clear that my predecessor wanted to hand over and get back to the bosom of his family before the end of the school summer holidays in September. To short-circuit the official period of hand-over, he suggested, it would be of mutual advantage if I came up to the Battalion for a few days during the language course, to get the hang of things and play myself into the task ahead.

Luckily this was in accord with the Language School policy of sending students to their ultimate destinations in order to practice the Arabic they had learnt so far. It also coincided with a mid-course break which enabled the instructors to have a short leave (or bone up on the next few weeks' lessons).

On 26 May, 1967, I flew up to Salalah, some nine hundred miles east of Aden, to visit the Muscat Regiment. As the plane circled the airfield I looked out of the window to view the terrain for which I would soon be militarily responsible. Beneath me the deep blue of the Indian Ocean merged suddenly with bright white surf pounding bright white sand. The town itself was a child's game of grey bricks, mud houses and dotted date palms, set in a wide crescent-shaped plain some fifty miles long; the plain clearly enclosed on the landward side by a forbidding range of mountains, black rock, purple and grey interspersed with green, incredible green, like Devon or Yorkshire.

Lieutenant-Colonel Trevor Alexander, my predecessor, my faithful correspondent, met me, a stocky, square-set figure wearing khaki cord trousers and a pale khaki shirt. On his head the blood-red tam-o'-shanter of the Muscat Regiment.. This incongruous form of head-dress for Arab soldiers originated in the Jebel War of 1956, when the Cameronians had been sent to assist the Sultan to quell the Imam's rebellion. Grateful for the Regiment's services and admiring their headgear the Sultan had then decreed that he would have the same design for his own senior regiment, but in the royal scarlet. There is to this day, presumably, some assiduous bonnet-maker in Scotland, turning out a regular quota of scarlet bonnets, mystified by the requirements of some lost Middle Eastern sect of a Highland clan.

Most RAF stations exude an air of desolation; of destruction real, impending or implied. RAF Salalah was the most desolate station I had yet encountered. Its tin-roofed, white-walled huts in orderly rows, its scattered false foliage, assiduously watered, its tennis courts and turquoise swimming pool, did little to offset the drab yellow sand and grey gravel, barbed wire and haphazard patches of oil which seemed to emerge from the continual heat haze and sand storm.

We drove in a long wheel-based Landrover along a rough stony track while Trevor's Baluchi orderly bounced about in the back, his round black face practically hidden by the folds of his shemag[10]. The fine white dust of that appalling road billowed up and around our progress and was to make the frequent journeys from the camp to Salalah a penance for months to come. Far to our left ran a dramatic grey escarpment of jagged rock rising abruptly from the edge of the plain. Through the shimmering heat haze this looked like an unbroken forbidden wall — in marked contrast to the glimpses of rolling grass-covered slopes behind and above it. The white scar of a rough track showed intermittently, zigzagging up the face of the Jebel.

"That's the Midway Road," said Trevor. "The only route to the north — into Rub al Khali, the Empty Quarter — and our only land route into the Oman proper."

"Who built it?"

"One of the oil companies — several have prospected here. Quite a feat. It's even worse on the northern edge of the Jebel. You'll see. They had to build a ramp there."

A dark low mass of ragged tents appeared through the dust before us; barbed wire and sandbagged emplacements, with sentries at the gate and in watch towers around the perimeter. The Landrover drew up beside a tent marked "Visitors" and I entered a small dark suffocating hole which contained a bed, a mosquito net, a camp chair, a table with a tin wash-basin on it and a jerrycan full of very hot water. The water had not been heated; it was just room temperature.

"Shake your shoes out before you put them on in the morning," said Trevor. "Scorpions. Dinner in half an hour." He departed.

"What about the loo?" I said.

He reappeared. "Ah, yes. Over there. I don't recommend that either. I go down to the RAF at Salalah for a shower every evening." Since the dust of the journey back was roughly equivalent to the dust accumulated on the outward run this seemed to me a fairly pointless exercise in motion without progress. I bathed in the tin basin.

Dinner was in the main Mess tent, two ragged, khaki marquees joined together, but there was nothing ragged about the food or service. Iced consommé, prawn cocktail, wild duck à l'orange and a bombe glacée were served by immaculate white-clad waiters presided over by Paul Gomez, the Mess Steward, servant and friend of the Regiment for many years. Because of a shortage of good cooks in Muscat the Sultan paid handsomely for stewards and cooks from Goa and thereby enabled the regiments of his Armed Forces to be justifiably proud of their messing. When there was little else to do but to train for and fight a small war, food became an important aspect of life.

Most of the Battalion was deployed in defensive positions on the Jebel but for special occasions all but one officer per company could be airlifted down to Battalion Headquarters. The guests, apart from myself, were pilots from the Sultan of Oman's Air Force (SOAF) seconded from the RAF, and the Military Secretary, a genial, Olympian figure called Brigadier Pat Waterfield. Waterfield had faithfully served the Sultan for some fifteen years, a most gifted and able man whose unhappy lot it was to say 'no' to most of the enormous number of demands on the Defence Budget.

For many years, under a nebulous Treaty of Friendship, Her Majesty's Government had been paying the Sultanate a subsidy of £1 million a year. This, in the untrammelled days of peace, was not notably inadequate.

With a battalion of infantry, a troop of artillery and various supporting elements and a sizeable part of the Air Force permanently deployed six hundred miles from their base in an active campaign against guerrilla rebels it was not enough. Moreover, at the first hint of discovery that oil could be produced in commercial quantities the British Government with indecent haste had discontinued the subsidy, leaving the Sultan to run the country from its own scant resources, accruing from the export of dates and dried fish, plus his own private fortune, until such time as oil revenues became a reality.

For this reason, at the time I joined the SAF, it was a pathetically ragged little army. The soldiers' shirts and denim trousers were torn and threadbare, their gym shoes worn and tied together with string. Many went barefoot. It said much for Waterfield's husbandry that we were rarely short of ammunition, weapons, petrol or rations.

Waterfield's appearances in officers' messes were, probably for this reason, fairly rare and on this occasion the officers, primed by good food and wine after long days of privation on the Jebel, pitched into him good and proper. The main argument centred around the need for helicopters. There were no roads in the Jebel and few areas where it was possible to take a vehicle of any sort. Movement in any direction was inhibited by precipitous wadis, strewn with giant boulders and dense thorn, many of which took twenty-four hours to cross, many impossible even for donkeys who carried vital weapons, ammunition and water, to negotiate.

The crying need for helicopters was for casualty evacuation. In this typical guerrilla war the enemy operated only in terrain favourable to himself, supported by the local tribes he had intimidated, terrain which was wildly inaccessible to conventionally-based security forces. Every foray to hunt him down meant a long approach march from the nearest base camp. When a company or patrol received casualties from a clash with the enemy the return journey was agonizingly slow, painful and dangerous.

Every officer had tales to tell of these long marches, with stretchers being man-handled down perpendicular slopes while a man's life blood dripped slowly away. Peter Raven, commanding C Company, was the most vociferous. In a recent ambush above the huge Wadi Jarsees, he had lost seven men, three of whom had sustained fairly straightforward gunshot wounds but had failed to survive the shock of the prolonged carry down the mountainside.

Waterfield took it all with genial off-handedness, pointing out the expense of running a helicopter force, the respective — and sometimes conflicting — merits of British, French and American makes and the other demands being made on the Exchequer. Would we prefer helicopters to, say, a rise in pay for Contract Officers? This was an astute riposte, well below the belt. The difference in pay and conditions between the Regular seconded officer and the contract officers (high-grade, experienced officers, but technically civilians, with no long-term career prospects in the Sultan's Forces) was a subject of endless controversy. Would we prefer helicopters instead of another hospital? Instead of another battalion of infantry, or jet aircraft, more pay to attract the recruits we so sorely needed? It was a matter of priorities.

I listened with mounting apprehension. Disregarding the highly emotional arguments for casualty evacuation by helicopter, I had heard enough to be certain that, from the wider operational point of view, even a limited number of helicopters would help to overcome most of the tactical problems of operating in that vast Jebel terrain. Properly used, they could increase by a factor of ten the effect of the troops and weapons at a commander's disposal. A small group of men, a mortar or medium machine gun lifted to a point behind or in flank of an enemy: supplies of all kinds, especially water, lifted to maintain troops on vital ground; information, a constant unblinking watch on enemy movements and strengths; casualty evacuation, not just to ease a man's pain or save his life but to obviate the waste of time and manpower needed to carry him back to base, aborting the whole carefully-planned operation, sapping our own morale while raising the enemy's.

There was nothing new in all this. Helicopters had been regarded as indispensable in every counter-insurgency campaign since 1948; in Malaya, Cyprus, Borneo, the Radfan, they had inspired an entirely new concept of operations, widening a commander's tactical options and vastly increasing his flexibility to react to the unforeseen. I lay awake in the hot dark hole of my tent enumerating the advantages of helicopters — just one; no, that would not be viable; one and one spare — they surely outweighed all the other priorities. When I left SAF three years later we were still operating without them.

The next morning we drove due north across the flat dusty plain. The grey-blue mass of the escarpment hung shimmering in the haze across our front, deceptively low, invitingly near. What appeared to be a ten-minute drive to the foothills took nearly an hour, the white scar of the Midway Road visible all the way. The thin layer of gravel on the Salalah plain enabled the Landrovers to be driven at forty miles per hour, each vehicle churning up a cloud of fine white dust in its wake, presenting a perfect target, telegraphing our approach to the rebels on the Jebel. Two long wheel-based Landrovers of the Reconnaissance Platoon escorted us, the soldiers facing outwards, rifles and LMGs ready for instant use, their heads swathed in red and white shemags.

"Bloody shemags make a frightful target," said Trevor. "We're supposed to be getting green ones but Waterfield probably lost the order."

It occurred to me that green ones would be as ineffective as red in the flat, khaki waste through which we were travelling but I said nothing. Soon the logic became apparent.

The road started slowly rising, taking the easiest route up the foothills of the main escarpment. Soon it rose more steeply, with acute hairpin bends and suddenly we were in a new world of lush green foliage, of jasmine and oleander and butterflies. The dull plain fell behind and below us; the air grew noticeably cooler. There was a faint sweet-smelling breeze. The track itself was a considerable feat of engineering, gouged out of a near solid rock precipice which necessitated constant changes of direction and gradient and produced seemingly endless hairpin bends. Every yard of the route provided perfect ambush positions and twice the mangled hulks of army vehicles reminded Trevor of past battles. Eighteen months later, when the war had entered a new phase, we had to fight to clear the rebels off this stretch of road as a matter of routine, but now, in June, 1967, the enemy were tired, ill-equipped and unaggressive, waiting for the massive assistance they expected to receive when the British got out of Aden.

The road straightened out and we were on top of the escarpment. Here the road makers must have sighed with relief as they followed a long plateau from south to north. Gentle, undulating slopes of long green grass were studded with rocky outcrops, thorn and frankincense bushes, but flanked on both sides by precipitous wadis, which sooner or later would swing east or west — and have to be traversed. From the first high point on the escarpment our destination was visible — painfully so. A cluster of white tents flapped shamelessly against the open green background in the middle distance and as we approached I was once more conscious of the difficulty of estimating time and distance in that vast country. It took us a further hour to reach the camp.

Derek Whittle, the Company Commander, met us, a large soft-spoken officer sporting a beard like W. G. Grace. After a few routine pleasantries he asked if we'd brought any sandwiches. Trevor handed over a cardboard box which had been placed in the Landrover by the Quartermaster, asked a few questions, said: "Well, I must be off," and departed the way we had come. A pretty abortive morning's work, I thought.

Derek led me over to his tent, outside which sat three smaller officers, with noticeably smaller beards; in fact one had just omitted to shave for two mornings. Tim Landon, the Reconnaissance Platoon commander, had resigned his commission in the 10th Hussars specifically to come to Muscat as a contract officer. He had a shy, unsmiling manner, a wry sense of humour, a lot of experience and spoke excellent Arabic. Dick Stacpoole had been a Colonial police officer in Zambia and Nick Roberts, seconded from the Blues & Royals, son of a General, had grown tired, like so many cavalry officers, of careering round the same training areas in a tank and volunteered for the Sultan's service.

They were all charming but the arrival of the future commanding officer clearly occasioned less interest than that of the sandwiches which they proceeded to demolish ravenously, washed down by warm beer. They offered me a packet wrapped in newspaper. The heat of the journey had long since dried them to a crisp but it was clearly all I was going to get so I did my best. I noticed, during this modest lunch, that it did not do to get too close to my brother officers. Companies averaged about a month on the Jebel without a break; water was short, temperatures in the nineties, the routine both hazardous and over-heating and laundry and clean clothes dependent on the irregular Landrover runs to Salalah. There was a very pungent odour as we squatted on our haunches in the midday sun; I wasn't sure if it was the officers or the sandwiches but I think on the whole I preferred the sandwiches.

After this slightly bizarre picnic we toured the company positions. These were encouraging. Each platoon was well sited, each man enclosed by a well-built sangar[11], each sentry alert and watching, finger on trigger. The men were brewing tea, heating mess tins of water on tiny hexamine cookers. They had curry for breakfast and curry for dinner. Tea was apparently all they had in the middle of the day.

I was there to practise my Arabic so I spoke to every man. They seemed genuinely interested to meet the prospective Colonel: "How are you? I am well, thanks be to God — How are you? Are you well? Are you content? Praise be to God! Is your health good? Thank God! How are you? I am well, thanks be to God." After these interminable greetings I asked them in meticulous Arabic how old they were, how long they had been in the Army, how many children they had, what the food was like. I was to discover that these were practically the sole topics of conversation one ever had with these soldiers, even after knowing them for some time. They were intrinsically polite and considerate so it may have been that, knowing the Colonel Sahib's limited conversational ability, they deliberately kept to a format that could be retained by a child of five. It was important that one shook hands, looked pleasant and said something; it didn't matter what. I have never lost this habit of greeting and have subsequently astounded young British soldiers by extending my hand at odd moments; some have visibly flinched.

I asked one man how old he was and he grinned hugely and said,

"One hundred and thirty". The truth was they didn't know how old they were. There was no way of telling and it didn't matter anyway, except for the strange insistence by the *gaysh*[12] that a man couldn't be expected to run or carry a rifle or march twenty miles in the sun after the age of thirty-five or so. When trying to establish where they lived one was bound to ask how many miles it was from Muscat, or Nizwa, or any reasonably prominent township. The answers to this sort of question were either an apologetic shrug of the shoulders — "M'arif"[13] or severely practical. Distances were invariably measured in time. The time would vary according to the mode of conveyance of the questioner. Thus a man in a Landrover would receive a different answer to a man on foot or camel. But the answers were fairly accurate.[14] Some of my questions were greeted with a smile of total incomprehension. When I asked one older man if he had understood, he smiled and explained that he didn't, that I spoke such beautiful, classical Arabic he was too humble and ignorant to understand it.

Every soldier sat cleaning his personal weapon, tenderly, slowly, rather than rushing it as a boring chore as British soldiers do, stripping, cleaning and oiling lovingly, for this rifle or light machine gun was the Government's greatest gift, a symbol of manhood, coveted since childhood. It was touching to see, in contrast, the ragged shirts and trousers, the threadbare gym shoes and the faded red shemags. The tents too were full of holes and leaked badly in the heavy rains. Again one heard the catalogue of the Defence Department's shortcomings.

The Company's task in this isolated Jebel position was not entirely clear to me, for Trevor had not explained his tactical concept. It seemed to provide a base from which patrols could search the deep wadis and scattered huts for rebels and also to give cover to the Midway Road. This was the one vital road link with northern Oman, the seat of Government, the administrative base and Force Headquarters. Had we had enough air or sea transport support we could have done without it, lifting men and material direct from Muscat to Salalah, but at this time it was essential to secure the land route for both reinforcement purposes and to sustain operations on the northern edge of the Jebel, east and west of the road. The cost in terms of men and time was high. No body of troops moved by day without carefully picqueting the high ground overlooking their route. If a Company had to do its own picqueting the rate of movement was painfully slow — and twice as hazardous, for it involved each picquet 'leap-frogging' over the next, covered by its fire onto successive pieces of dominating ground. Meanwhile the main force had to delay its advance, for to move without this elementary precaution invited disaster. It was therefore the practice when possible to pre-position the Company or Companies as a covering force on or near the routes to be followed, which could provide the picquets, and this was one of B Company's main tasks on the Midway Road.

This brief excursion into the operational area of the Regiment was all I had time for. Two days later I flew back to Aden to complete my language course. From my brief visit on the Jebel I retained four general impressions: the terrain was vast; we must have helicopters; the rebels were comparatively dormant; the officers were ill fed and the soldiers ill-clothed and ill-equipped.

The size and character of the terrain was daunting. Flying over the operational area to the west of B Company's position I had seen totally different country to the rolling green uplands of the Midway Road. This was known as "Moon Country" — miles of rugged gravel desert, continually ridged and pock-marked changing in the morning light from mauve to bright yellow, featureless for miles, then suddenly traversed by black, shadowy canyons; dense thorn forests growing out of solid rock, huge boulders poised crazily at the top of cavernous wadis or littering its sides as if scattered by a mad giant; 25,000 square miles of terrain which made the deserts of North Africa and the mountains of Italy in their vastness at least predictable. Here a man might have to fight in at least three different kinds of country in a single day — flat sand, dense thorn and mountains. How could a battalion exist in such country without aircraft to drop them water or massive animal transport to carry food and weapons? How could a battalion cover such an area if the rebels gained in number and strength? A division, a corps would be lost in that colossal playground.

The rebels were clearly not particularly aggressive at this time and they rarely attacked an alert and tactically well-found body of SAF (this was true of every guerrilla) but we could take no liberties with them. Moreover, the position would surely deteriorate after the final British withdrawal from Aden in six months' time, when all sorts of useful arms, ammunition and equipment would be handed over to the Adenis who would no doubt dispense much of it to neighbouring 'freedom fighters'. The thought of B Company's isolated position if the rebels brought up a few medium machine guns one night was frightening.

Food: two officers had already been invalided home with ulcers. Derek Whittle was nursing one and Dick Stacpoole looked gaunt. (He was evacuated with a kidney complaint within a fortnight). The officers must be made to eat properly while on the Jebel. The Arab soldier's basic fare could not sustain a European.

Helicopters and equipment, Allah, oil revenues and Waterfield would doubtless provide in due course. We must get priorities right. My brain was so busy as I returned to Aden I almost failed to notice the discomfort of the flight.

It was late June. The course ground slowly to a halt, the language laboratory and its air-conditioning plant failing at the same moment. I passed both the written and oral examinations and collected a bounty of £104 less tax from a grateful government. I visited the British Military Hospital, practising my Arabic once again, this time on two SAF soldiers severely wounded by mortar fire, and departed impressed by their cheerful fatalism and lack of bitterness. One had lost his right hand; of particular significance to the Arab.

The massacre of 5th Fusiliers and Argylls described earlier had occurred on 29 June. The Argylls continued their expert domination of Crater while the withdrawal of British troops and air forces was carried out in an orderly manner and the people of Aden became more hopelessly involved in the mindless morass of bitterness and incompetence that was to emerge as the People's Republic of South Yemen.

Somewhat shamefully I returned to Britain to see my children and play some polo before returning to Muscat for two and a half years.

5

A dramatic change had taken place in the quarters of the Muscat Regiment since I had visited them in May. They had moved into the first permanent garrison buildings ever constructed for the army in Dhofar. In place of the tented camp on the drab, mosquito-ridden plain there now rose a neat, purpose-built battalion barracks. Instead of the tattered, sagging khaki tents (accommodation scale — 8 men and one officer) stood rows of pristine, white concrete barrack blocks with windows which opened and closed and electric ceiling fans, each room within a hundred yards of its shared ablution facilities. True, these wash-houses were nothing more than concrete outhouses containing a communal tap and a huge cement container, like a sheep-dip, in which men could wash themselves, their clothes and their bedding. The lavatories' incongruous white china pedestals with pull-chain flushes, were less successful. The native soldiers were unable to break the habit of centuries, whereby stones were used in this daily function instead of paper and the drainage system was unable to cope with such violation. Already, a few weeks after the ceremonial opening, the doors to these temples of hygiene were wired up and the soldiers continued to defecate outside the camp's wire perimeter. This practice was less unhygienic than might be supposed for the sun baked their efforts in half a day and an army of beetles and flies purified them in half a minute. An officer's mess, twenty cell-like rooms with blessed air conditioning which roared like a factory, and showers en suite, were built round an elongated patch which Richard John had already planted with bright orange zinnias and reluctant grass. The Headquarters complex, with its bright Beau Geste tower and fortress walls

47

brooded benignly over all, the Sultan's plain red flag proclaiming sovereignty over its desolate surroundings. Umm al Ghawarif — the Mother of the Mosquito — bade you welcome.

Into the Commanding Officer's office of this complex, there entered on my first day a diminutive Arab boy, in spotless white dishdasha and round skullcap. After the usual interminable Arab greetings he announced, "I am Yahya, in charge of tea arrangements."

Later, John Cooper told me about him. He had been a mess boy with the Regiment at Nizwa, under age and under size, even for that undemanding station in life. Nobody knew how old he was and Yahya wasn't telling. No soldiers or camp followers under the age of sixteen were allowed to serve in Dhofar and Yahya was reluctantly told that he would not be able to accompany the Regiment when it moved south. He was welcome to stay on as a mess boy with the incoming regiment at Nizwa and could of course graduate, when he was old enough and if Allah was good enough to let him grow to the requisite height, to combative ranks in the army in the fullness of time. Yahya refused to be mollified by this distant prospect and spent much of his time appealing against the decision. The authorities remained adamant. When the impressive convoy of trucks and Landrovers left Nizwa for the six-hundred-mile drive south to Dhofar, each vehicle carried two or three burmails (petrol drums) of fresh water for the desert journey. At the first halt on the first evening, one of the drivers was amazed to discover a grimy, and sand-covered Yahya, near exhaustion, peering at him from one of the burmails. Such persistence could not be rebuffed and Yahya stayed, an outstanding purveyor of tea and office orderly, throughout the tour of the south.

A round-faced, circular Baluchi orderly ushered me into the small bungalow allotted to the commanding officer and fussed over my kit. Lance Corporal Suleiman Dad Karim spoke no English but his whole military life was apparently dedicated to anticipating my every whim, thus making communication more or less superfluous. When bidding me goodnight he would stand uncertainly in the doorway and mutter "Shay-ee?" I have never drunk early morning tea in my life, preferring to savour the last moments in bed undisturbed, but no self-respecting orderly in the Sultan's Armed Forces had yet encountered a British sahib who faced the day unfortified by a cup of tea, so from that moment on I acquiesced in the order for tea, adding the hour at which I wished to be woken. Quite frequently this was one or two in the morning, to go on an operation of some sort; sometimes it was at three in the afternoon, but I never learnt the Arabic for "Wake me up but do not bring tea," so for two and a half years I was called with a cup of tea which never got drunk.

The three rifle companies of the battalion were disposed much as they had been when I came up from Aden; one on the Midway Road, covering the vital land route linking Dhofar with the rest of the country; one due west, above the escarpment, at Janook; a half company at Mughsail on the coast west of Salalah and the bare minimum of half a company in camp as a reserve. The positions deployed west of Salalah — B Company at Janook and a half A at Mughsayl — were designed to cover the routes into Dhofar from the Aden Protectorate, from which the Dhofar Liberation Front was being increasingly nourished. Marxist elements over the border were already building the supply and training network which was to sustain the Dhofari rebels through thirteen long years of war and it clearly made sense to deploy as many of our own resources as we could afford to gain information on this movement and if possible to disrupt it. A glance at the map or, worse, a reconnaissance flight by Beaver light aircraft, showed how forlorn these resources were. Hundreds of camel tracks running from west to east were clearly visible threading through thickly wooded mountainous country, through which scores of men, material and animals could move undetected.

One and a half companies, perhaps a hundred and fifty men, was a hopelessly inadequate force to provide information on any movement in such a huge area, let alone inhibit it in any way. The focal point of this movement, midway between the tree line and the open desert to the north, where most of the established camel tracks were alleged to converge, was at Janook, manned by B Company.

The small single-handed Beaver took off from the rough strip at Umm al Ghawarif camp and flew due west. In the clear dawn air the extent of the battalion's operational area became dauntingly clear. We climbed gently over the crescent-shaped Salalah plain, clearly bounded on our left by the glaring beaches and deep blue sea of the Indian Ocean, on our right by the grey mass of the escarpment, its four-thousand-foot wall split at intervals by precipitous wadis running broadly from north to south into the green plateau of the Qara mountains. Somewhere down there in the Wadi Naheez, which looked even from this height like the Grand Canyon, had died Captain Alan Woodman, one of our predecessors, a bullet in his stomach, reporting his fatal ambush on the wireless, urging the reinforcements to hurry as the light was going. But it was still midday and broad daylight . . . Hamish Emslie had been ambushed on the high ground further north. A 3.5 inch rocket launcher knocked out his Landrover, killing all the occupants.

The pilot circled laboriously to gain height and we were over the escarpment at its western end, over trees and scrub and rolling downland, again broken by massive wadis and rocky outcrops. To our far right, where the monsoon rains ended like a curtain, the flat open desert was visible, dissolving in the haze of the Empty Quarter to the north. I gazed gloomily at this apparently limitless territory, for whose security I was apparently solely responsible. Surely this whole area could harbour a thousand terrorists in perpetual camel convoy, even moving by daylight beneath that canopy of low trees, from the main rebel base at Hauf, safely over the border, into the central Jebel above Salalah. But I was assured that they moved only in the tree line to the south, that comparatively narrow corridor of cover between the sea and the open 'moon country' to the north. Even a small convoy, a single camel, could be spotted in the open by the Sultan's Air Force. Theoretically, any suspicious movement could then be intercepted by ground forces, but I had severe doubts about the practicality of such a move. The treeline, with its canopy of cover and numerous water holes, was the key. Gradually, as we flew west, the tree line gave way to sparse scrub and then the grey irregular slopes and wadis of the 'moon country', dusty, waterless gravel where the tracks of the centuries were a maze of conflicting directions, blocked by cavernous wadis every few yards. This even the bedu avoided in their seasonal wanderings, a desolation — no shelter, no shade, no water, no grazing.

Suddenly we dipped down to land in an open desert strip about three miles north of the company camp at Janook. Derek Whittle,

1. Anthony Lort-Phillips, Guy Sheridan, Peter Thwaites and Martin Sullivan attending the CO's briefing before Operation Lance.

2. Guy Sheridan, Richard Kinsella-Bevan, Peter Thwaites and Simon Sloane returning, dirty and exhausted, to Defa.

3. On top of the Jebel, looking towards the Yemen border.

4. Brigadier Corran Purdon presenting the Sultan's Commendation to Major John Cooper at Bid Bid.

5. Peter Thwaites in audience with His Highness Sultan Said bin Taimur.

6. Operations round Wadi Jardoom. Peter Thwaites, Richard Kinsella-Bevan, Simon Sloane and Guy Sheridan.

7. Guy Sheridan, Simon Sloane and Richard Kinsella-Bevan snatching a quick meal before stand-to and a night march out of the enemy area during Operation Lance.

8. Simon Sloane interrogating a Jebali after a dawn cordon and search on the Jebel.

the large, bearded officer I had last seen with his company at the Midway Road met me. The Landrover was stripped of its superstructure and windscreen, its floor covered with sandbags as protection against mines. It was filthy, scarred and dented and any one of its grinding, shuddering jolts would, I thought, finish it long before any mines. The few tents of the camp were as ragged as I remembered them and the men's clothing and equipment, like the transport, near the end of their useful life, but every soldier was alert and purposeful, well protected by a stone sangar and constantly, lovingly nursing his rifle or machine gun.

The rebels in this area were quiescent and rarely observable, but one could not take liberties with them. Their intelligence on SAF movements, based on local bedu and female goatherds, was sharper than ours and a weak patrol acting carelessly would immediately become a target, as Derek had found to his cost; but a force of ten to fifteen men, alert and moving professionally, though watched by the enemy unseen, would survive unharmed. The main pre-occupation was to inhibit enemy movement through the company area and this was achieved by day and night patrols and ambush parties lying up in the low scrub which marked the beginning of the treeline to the south of the position.

B Company had started to build a track to an observation point perched on top of the escarpment some ten miles to the south and we marched there the next day. The view was breathtaking. The gradually sloping ground suddenly fell away in the rocky cliff of the escarpment and we gazed down upon fold after fold of thickly wooded slopes, bright green and hazy in the morning sun, down to the coastal village of Rakhyut, one of the westernmost outposts of the Sultanate, and beyond to the deep blue ocean.

This was the place to be if we wanted to dominate the western approaches to the Sultanate; here on this rocky outcrop was the vital ground from which the routes through the treeline could be overlooked. True, during the three months of the monsoon movement would be screened by both mist and low cloud and in the month immediately following by the low thick foliage of the trees, but later, from October to June, the scrub would be thin and brown. Derek called the place Everest and he was wise to see its potential for surveillance and to build a track so that men and supplies could be deployed there.

A Company at Mughsail was deployed further east, some thirty miles west of Salalah, with the same aim of inhibiting rebel movement along the same camel tracks still further east where they debouched onto the Salalah plain or wound their way north into the central Jebel. But here the treeline was broader, not so dense but stretching north deeper into the escarpment and beyond. The company's base was dictated by the only available water supply, a brackish fresh water inlet running down to the sea. Thus restricted, the Company's radius of operations was limited to the distance they could march on the water they could carry. Dropping water by air was feasible but immediately compromised their position. There was thus a huge area to the north of A Company which they could not cover.

That was it. The remaining company, C, was in reserve in camp, its strength dissipated by local guards and convoy protection duties. Once again the pitiful inadequacy of troops to cover the tasks, in an operational area the size of Wales, overwhelmed me. While the rebels remained unadventurous and unaggressive, this was not critical but once they were reinforced and resupplied and gained in strength and initiative — and they were far from being beaten — the situation would deteriorate dramatically.

Bob Brown, the Intelligence Officer, was not optimistic. The acquisition of intelligence depended on many factors; local informers, casually rewarded for their information, regular agents or "sources" on the permanent payroll; ex-rebels who had surrendered or been captured and been "turned". The informants, whether regular or casual, tended to receive payment whatever information they offered, and much of it was valueless or even false. The ex-rebels at this time had long since left the DLF and their information, at least on the vital matter of current rebel movements, tended to be out of date.

The real incentive for timely and accurate intelligence was missing — morale, a national or at least local impetus to rid the area of unrest. Generally speaking, the Dhofari was apathetic towards the Sultan's needs. They regarded him, indeed they regarded every Omani, as an interloper whose family had come down from the north to help settle their tribal affairs but had outstayed his welcome. He was a recluse they hardly saw and his rule was harsh and uncaring. There was some sympathy for these rebels. They only wanted a better deal for the Dhofaris, a lifting of the more repressive regulations. Why could they not leave the Sultanate for business or education, and then return, without being banished for ever? Why was there such severe restriction on owning a vehicle in a country where huge distances had to be covered? Why so few schools and hospitals? Why was music forbidden, sun-glasses prohibited? Why was a man not permitted an electric pump instead of the laborious hand pump, to coax water from the unforgiving sand and rock? Why a law against transistor radios?

There were of course good reasons for many of these apparently unnecessary restrictions. Although the presence of oil had been discovered and plans were going ahead to develop it, no actual revenue was likely to be received for many months and the economy was still paralysed by a niggardly national income. Money was simply not available to build the roads, hospitals and schools so desperately needed. As to the electric pumps, the Sultan had been advised that the water table — in the few places where there was water — was limited and the supply would not withstand the demands that would be imposed by automatic pumps. Transistor radios, so easily available across the border and through the Gulf, merely facilitated reception of the subversive and revolutionary voice of Cairo, urging the people to throw off the yoke of Imperialism and its Arab stooges. But the people could not be expected to understand these restrictions and no attempt was made to explain them. And thus the seeds of the revolt took root and flourished and more and more peaceful and acquiescent citizens, both in Dhofar and Oman, muttered their opposition to the Sultan's rule.

The Battalion was due to return to northern Oman in November, a few weeks away. In these last few weeks of our operational tour I was anxious to achieve some measure of operational success. The British Government had finally surrendered its position in Aden, at the opposite end of the Arabian Peninsula, and the last troops were being withdrawn, leaving a tenuous alliance of up-country Sheikhs threatened by the markedly left-wing NLF and the terrorist Marxist FLOSY. I was convinced that the Dhofari rebels would have built up their strength, supported by the Marxists, by the time we came south for our next tour and I needed to learn all I could at this last opportunity.

Bob Brown remained justifiably gloomy about the accuracy of his Intelligence. For some time there had been low-grade reports of a group of rebels living in the Jebel Harr area, a high broad plateau to the east of Taqa.

"The trouble is I haven't got a Fred from that area," he said. Fred was the name given to each of the former rebels who now acted as guides and informers with the SAF. There was Fred One, Fred Two — and that, at the time, was the sum total of Freds. Fred Two, however, before yielding to the blandishments of the DLF recruiting officer, had been the Government honey collector and knew the Jebel Harr better than most. "He won't want to go because it's monsoon and he hates getting wet."

This was a fairly general aversion. It was not just the cold and unremitting drizzle; the Jebel was shrouded in thick mist from dawn to dusk. This made control difficult and an enemy ambush all too easy. However, it seemed to me worth doing a reconnaissance in force of the area which Bob thought would eventually merit a large-scale operation. It would enable me to see how companies operated at first hand, to get to know the terrain over which I was clearly going to operate on many future occasions and, most important, to gain personal knowledge of the type of operation of which I had little experience. I had some experience of operations in the jungles of Malaya, the Cameroons and British Guiana and of the open desert of Egypt, but the complexity and sheer size of the Dhofar terrain seemed to be unique.

I decided to use Peter Raven's C Company, the only company under my hand in camp at that time, as well as half of A Company which could be withdrawn temporarily from Mughsail, accepting the risk that this route would thereby be uncovered for a time. The plan was to approach the target area from two sides, west and east, silently by night, to halt the half company in a suitable stop line in concealed positions and to search towards them with the other company, hoping that any enemy would stand and fight or withdraw on to the ambush line. It was exactly the same principle as a partridge drive over a wide area. The operation, like so many of its kind, was to prove almost completely abortive, a waste of time, energy and manpower, but not, on this occasion, of life and limb.

I moved with C Company, making it quite clear to the Company Commander that I was a passenger, would do what I was told and would not interfere once the operation was launched. Peter Raven was an extremely competent officer with years of experience from Korea and with 22 SAS in the Malayan Emergency.

We motored across desert tracks, eastwards and roughly parallel to the coastal track, without lights, through Taqa and well beyond the area in which we wished to deploy, in order to mislead the enemy who could overlook, from the escarpment, the whole of our route. We debussed some eight miles to the east of our objective and marched silently back to a point below the escarpment from which we would climb to the plateau above. It rained solidly the whole time. At about two in the morning we put out sentries and lay down to sleep where we stood. At four we rose, shivering in our damp clothing and equipment, shook out into formation and started to climb. We were blind in the dark and, after dawn, we were blind in the damp, close, swirling mist which reduced visibility to about five yards. The soft, red soil, short turf and rocky outcrops made the going so slippery it was difficult to remain upright and in the steepest places one step forwards was followed inevitably by a slither of two paces backwards. The conditions were the worst possible for a large-scale reconnaissance requiring stealth, silence and unobtrusive movement.

We climbed doggedly for six or seven hours, which took us to a height of about three thousand feet. I had insisted on wireless silence until we were well into the area where the rebels lived or until surprise was lost. At the appointed time we opened up and, encouragingly, spoke to A Company, who sounded very close and were as impotent in the mist as we were. Only at one point was there a sign of enemy presence. Peter Raven, a couple of yards in front of me, held up his hand and we froze to listen. The shadowy figures we felt rather than saw slipped down the gully to our left, totally soundless and a moment later we blundered into the few mud huts which had sheltered them.

The weather was clearly not going to improve. With more experience I would learn that this was typical *hareef* (monsoon) weather: a thick scotch mist more or less continuously accompanied by thin drizzling rain. It would not improve later in the day. It would not improve for months.

We halted on the steep, short shelf of the mountain, still shrouded in mist, still listening to the plaintive voice of A Company's wireless operator, similarly baffled and blinded . . . where? So near-sounding but probably across a wadi a mile away. We nibbled gloomily on chapattis like brown blotting paper, drank cold tea from our water bottles and marched onwards by a different route.

At one of our halts I noticed some succulent mushrooms sprouting from the damp green grass and picked a few. Suleiman Dad Karim, a hillman like most Baluchis, grinned for the first time that day and set about picking them conscientiously, putting them gently in his *shemag* like a shopping bag. By now the slope was treacherously slippery, far more so going gown than going up and first one and another of this punitive expedition fell head over heels. We all wore either gym shoes or rubber-soled desert boots and these gave no grip. The operation descended into pure farce. At one point everyone in sight was spreadeagled, weapons and equipment flying. Omani soldiers are great gigglers and to a man they had collapsed laughing. I barked at them sternly to control themselves, but the words dissolved in the mist as I somersaulted on my back. As I went down I caught sight of Dad Karim, literally in midair, feet uppermost, his *shemag* held high to protect the mushrooms. He was cackling with laughter.

The whole operation was almost totally valueless, except to impress on me the difficulty of operating in the monsoon, the lack of visibility and the need for tight control, the vulnerability. And, but for the mushrooms . . .

Another two or three weeks passed before Bob Brown considered the intelligence ripe for another sortie against the Jebel Harr. Apparently the rebel group remained in the area, perhaps observing the principle that lightning rarely strikes twice in the same place. In fact, of course, they lived there, had plenty of warning of any significant body of troops advancing across the open ground to operate against them and were not going to leave their traditional grazing grounds because of the occasional sorties against them.

Thus, there followed operation "Final Fling" involving all the forces ground and air, at my disposal, an account of which forms the first chapter of this book. I wrote out the statutory five copies of the report of this operation for Force Headquarters in Muscat and forwarded a copy to the Sultan in his Palace in Salalah. In due course I was summoned to his presence.

The palace was magnificently sited on the sea shore, its stone walls separated it from by the thunderous surf of the Indian Ocean, a low sea wall and fifty yards of dazzling white sand. Every entrance gate and courtyard was guarded by a pair of ancient cannon and manned by a group of picturesque but mostly overweight slaves carrying Martini-Henry rifles. Sheikh Hamid bin Hamood, a cousin of the Sultan who acted as his secretary, met me at the outer gate. He invariably wore a brown, gold embellished *biht*[15] with a white turban. He spoke only in Arabic in a hoarse, rasping voice and was unfailingly courteous, seeing much, betraying nothing. He led the way, bowing and pausing every few steps, through long stone passages and up stone flights of stairs, finally ushering me into a small, ugly office, grey painted, austerely furnished. No rare oriental carpets or silken walls relieved its gloom; oil cloth and machine-made rugs from Pakistan covered the floor. Modern, angular, plastic-covered chairs were arranged round the large desk, empty save for the chrome model of a modern aircraft, behind which sat His Highness Said bin Taimur Sultan of Muscat and Oman.

Who is the Sultan, the Sultan of Oman?

Is he a Yes-Man or a No-Man?

Is he a pro — or anti Status Quo man?

Is he noblest, like the Roman?

Or is he abominable, like the snowman?

So ran the rather irreverent rhyme which coursed through the corridors of power when events in the comparatively unknown Sultanate burst upon the public scene at the time of the Jebel War in 1956.

A small, neat, rather dumpy figure stood courteously to greet me, extending a velvet soft and richly scented hand. Brown eyes twinkled warmly above a brown mouth, embellished by a long, white beard untrimmed in the Moslem fashion. He wore a simple white *dishdash*[16] and a white turban.

"How do you do?" Each syllable was carefully pronounced but without a trace of accent. The voice was musical and well pitched. He gestured to a plastic-covered chair, then sat at his desk. There was a silence. He was perfectly relaxed and stared at me amiably. There was much I wanted to say. Here was the source of all power and influence in my life at that moment. I knew however it would be impolite to come straight to the point.

"How are your men?"

"Well, thank you, Sir. Looking forward to going back to their families." Oh! That could be taken as an insult, a disinclination to serve their Sultan in Dhofar. But he saw the point.

"Of course."

He seemed to be waiting for me to take the initiative, so I plunged.

"We had a useful operation in the Jebel Harr, Sir."

He nodded slowly. "I was interested in your report. I heard several of the adoo were killed."

This was news to me. Our intelligence had reported only two wounded.

"I'm sorry we had to burn some of the houses."

"You should have burned them all. They are bad people."

Another long pause.

"Had you thought of getting any helicopters, Sir?"

"They are very expensive."

"Of course, but they would enable us to make better use of our limited number of troops by getting behind the enemy unexpectedly, by supplying them in awkward places and by lifting heavy weapons about the Jebel."

"I see."

"They would also save lives, because at present it takes so long to get the wounded down from the Jebel, they often die from shock on the way."

"I see."

I had been told about His Highness's response to most advice. "I see" tended to dispose of the topic in hand. It meant: "I hear what you say but will think about it/don't agree/don't intend to do anything about it now."

Another long pause. There were other matters to discuss. I plunged on and briefed the Sultan on the military situation.

"How is your family?" he said.

My predecessor had warned me that this signified the end of official discussion and heralded a short period of small talk. A huge slave brought two glasses of fresh lime juice on a silver salver. I drank it as quickly as good manners allowed, bowed and left.

Preparations for the move north were well in hand, for our year's tour in Dhofar was at an end and we were to be relieved by the newly formed Desert Regiment, commanded by an Irish Guardsman called Brian Barnes, like myself seconded from the Household Brigade. There was, however, one more operational concept I wanted to try before we moved north. It was obvious that operations involving the concentration of the whole battalion, as in "Final Fling", tended to prejudice surprise of the enemy, and that even approaching by night march a successful contact would need accurate intelligence (which we always lacked) or the greatest luck. In their current state of low morale (which we all expected would be short-lived) the rebels would clearly do their utmost to lie low and avoid detection by superior forces.

Perhaps then the small, fast-moving, hard-hitting patrol might succeed where the unwieldy battalion force failed. My operations officer, Peter Southwood-Hayton, had long been an advocate of a fighting patrol of eight to ten picked men, each one a marksman, equipped with automatic weapons, wireless, the lightest of rations and a blanket each, moving like Jebalis through likely rebel areas.

It seemed worth a try and Peter and Tim Landon (the second-in-command of C Company), who spoke the weird guttural patois of the Jebalis, volunteered to train and lead the force. The main danger was, of course that they would be overwhelmed by a superior concentration of rebels and have no reserves or heavy weapons to get them out of trouble. If they had a casualty, too, they would have difficulty both carrying him and protecting themselves. On balance, I thought it was worth the risk. No recent rebel sightings had involved parties of rebels more than half a dozen strong.

I gave them specific instructions to take no risks, to move by night whenever possible, to gain information by stealth and to engage the enemy only in smaller numbers than themselves. Even so it was an enterprise full of risks and one which should never have been tried against a more aggressive or well-organized enemy.

In the event, they marched for some twenty miles into the Jebel before Tim Landon badly sprained his ankle and they turned for home. But the ruse worked. In the mist they passed within a few feet of a group of rebels, moving in single file along the same track, each group more surprised than the other. They answered the traditional greeting and prepared to fire their weapons from under the blankets around their shoulders. Suddenly the leading rebel shouted, "*Gaysh*" and, as a man, the group fled into the mist.

The venture had the advantage of keeping the rebels guessing, of proving that the Sultan's Forces were likely to be met anywhere, in any guise or strength. It proved that we could get really close to the rebels in spite of their reluctance to be engaged, perhaps to snatch a vital prisoner. But the whole concept was risky and I felt that once the enemy had built up strength, reinforced from a "liberated" Aden Protectorate, we would never be able to try it again.

The handover to the Desert Regiment, tactically, company by company, went smoothly ahead. Our relief looked a fearsome lot as they streamed down from the north in their stripped-down Landrovers, bristling with machine guns, officers and men bearded like Dervishes. When I took over the Muscat Regiment, steeped in a long tradition of clean-shaven combat in my own regiment, I had forbidden beards to be worn by the British officers — much to the annoyance of those who argued that they were good camouflage, helped to prevent desert sores and saved vital water on the Jebel. Some British officers even contended that the facial hair made them indistinguishable from the Arab soldiers and therefore less of a target.

It was my view that any self-respecting Jebali could spot a European six hundred yards away, beard or no beard, that a daily shave was good for discipline and morale and that adequate ablutions, including a shave, could be had on half a mug of water, in which you had already cleaned your teeth. Anyway, British beards looked scruffy. No beards. Now, in the early stages of the handover I heard one of my officers tell a bearded brigand in the Desert Regiment, "The Muscat Regiment don't wear beards."

On our last day in Dhofar Tony Carey took the Recce platoon along the coast road to Mirbat, to show the DR officers the route, which lay dangerously close to the escarpment and through the numerous likely and proven enemy ambush positions. In spite of careful picqueting (whereby dominating ground was occupied ahead of the main body) they managed to be ambushed, the enemy hitting both the front and rear ends of the convoy of Landrovers simultaneously. They called up the ever-ready strike aircraft and scampered willingly into the undergrowth to flush out the adoo, but they, having fired their first disruptive salvoes, had fled. It was lucky they were, at that time, such rotten shots. The legend that hawk-eyed Arab tribesmen were deadly marksmen was, mercifully, a myth. In spite of a great weight of automatic fire from British-made Bren guns, only one man was wounded.

There was one more visit to the Palace. I had been warned that if a battalion pleased the Sultan during its tour of duty, he was graciously pleased to hand over large sums of baksheesh to the soldiers. (It was not invariable; if His Highness was displeased a battalion got nothing.) But when I was invited to present myself at the Palace with a large truck and an armed escort I felt reasonably hopeful. With the minimum of ceremony Sheikh Hamid bin Hamood, aided by various beefy slaves, loaded on to my truck canvas sacks of freshly minted rupees, enough to award every officer and soldier several months pay.

The Sultan thanked me generously and said the battalion had done well. He then presented me with a gold wrist-watch which, after only three months service, I felt I had done little to deserve. I still have it.

6

The convoy fanned out across the khaki desert plain, each vehicle making its own route and best speed (which was mostly flat out), those on the far flank just specks in the shimmering haze, each trailing a scarf of dust and sand.

My sense of strict convoy discipline, nurtured in other, more conventional theatres of mock war, was outraged; thirty mph, twenty-two vehicles to the mile, regular spacing; endless halts and hang-ups. But there was method in this mad rush. The top two or three inches of the desert was a thin crust of gravel, level and just firm enough to bear the weight of one laden three-tonner, travelling fast. Successive vehicles in the same track would sink through into a fine, powdery sand and be reduced to a crawl in low gear, high ratio, engine and gearbox overheating and finally grinding to a halt. Moreover we had six hundred and forty miles to go. We carried with us all our weapons, equipment and baggage (and each soldier brought an astonishing personal load of dried fish, fresh fruit and vegetables available only in Dhofar) as well as all the fuel, rations (live chickens and goats on the hoof) and water needed for the journey. The longer we took on the march the greater these loads would need to be.

And so we rushed on like some monstrous cavalry charge, steering on a rough compass bearing but following the maze of old vehicle tracks which would scar the desert for fifty years. At dusk we halted, for the soldiers would pray as the sun sank in a fierce red ball below the horizon and the air cooled dramatically and fires sprang up round each group of vehicles. (Firewood from Dhofar formed a large part of our load, too.) I walked round the battalion while

Murad, the driver, tinkered with some Landrover engines and Dad Karim warmed some water for washing.

Paul Gomez, the Goanese Officers' Mess Steward, was issuing sharp instructions to the Mess boys, all of them covered with a fine crust of sand and sweat, clothes, hair, faces, so that they all looked like little gingerbread men as they bustled about preparing dinner. First, two trestle tables, stark in the sand, then a miraculously white table-cloth, cutlery, glasses, chairs. Then Paul changed rapidly into his white shirt, trousers and cummerbund, to preside over the faultless service of crayfish cocktail, roast chicken and fresh fruit salad, washed down with an iced white Chianti.

For subsequent meals, as ice melted and fresh food ran out, the cuisine would deteriorate to all-in stew and warm lager, but this first dinner, two hundred miles into the desert, was a thing to remember, of drowsy voices and glowing cigars in the warm dusk, while the soldiers joked and sang harsh repetitive songs round their fires and the night sky lightened in a blaze of stars.

A short night's sleep and by dawn, still shivering and bleary-eyed, we had covered fifty miles. The desert stretched endlessly in all directions, for our route lay along the south-eastern limits of the Rub al Khali, the Empty Quarter, which stretches some twelve hundred miles into Saudi Arabia and the Emirates to the north. This was the Great Sand Sea, crossed by Bertram Thomas in 1935 and by Thesiger in 1945 in their lonely camel convoys, and, more recently, in Ford trucks by the Saudi-backed rebels of the Dhofar Liberation Front in 1965.

For three days we saw no sign of life but that of our own convoy and, once, two distant gazelle fleeing from our harsh invasion. We came to Haima, a brackish well, where the early oil prospectors had made a camp, now a ghost town of empty, rotting huts and desert flotsam halfway to the foothills of the north.

The Wahiba sands, where Peter Raven's company on their way south a year ago had caught a young silver oryx, that rare Arabian breed whose straight horns, sometimes merged into a single shaft, gave life to the legend of the unicorn. The oryx became a regimental mascot. For hundreds of miles we passed only flat gravel, soft sand, low rocky outcrops and bushes of dwarf palm or acacia scrub, until on the evening of the third day the ground rose into more frequent rocky foothills, occasional sand dunes and palm-fringed villages. And all over, first as a dark smudge on the horizon, then as some grey, brooding backcloth to our whole vision, the great massif of the Jebel Akhdar range, the Green Mountain of northern Oman. Here we struck a graded sand track — the main trunk road of Oman connecting Nizwa, the ancient capital of the interior — with the Batinah Coast and Muscat itself.

There is a tradition widely held in the Army that your own particular unit invariably hands over its camp or barracks to its successors pristine and in immaculate order, only to take over elsewhere from its predecessors, as they move on, a camp of such startling squalor and neglect that the habits and antecedents of the previous occupants are immediately called into question. Thus it was that we found Bid Bid camp in bad order, the barrack huts dirty and ill-painted, the paths and flower beds unkept, the Officers' Mess a travesty of civilized living and good taste. No doubt the Desert Regiment, on taking over our clean and well-ordered accommodation in Salalah, that subtly tasteful ambience of our mess, felt precisely the same.

We settled in. The soldiers went on leave, many of them to the families they had not seen for a year. Meanwhile, rear parties cleaned and painted, carted truckloads of fine grey gravel from the wadis to make roads and paths and terraces, together with subsoil from the Batinah to coax fruit and flowers from the sand and rock. John Cooper, the tireless second-in-command, planted avenues of young acacia down every road in the camp and built a water garden on the natural shelf of the Officers' Mess garden, overlooking the Wadi Bid Bid. Here we sat in the cool evenings, contemplating the wide grey wadi with its thick belt of date palms and shallow meandering water, the far bank rising in the precipitous volcanic face of the Hajar mountains. Here we sat, swaddled in blankets after dinner, while the latest films were shown and the soldiers gathered round in the darkness cheering when the US Cavalry arrived in the nick of time and exhibiting naked Arab racism with their cries of 'Sharbash, Sambo!"[16] when the negro got to kiss the blonde heroine.

My bungalow was at one end of the Officers' Mess garden, a sitting room, two bedrooms and a bathroom, and it was here, when I departed on Christmas leave that the wives of three officers descended, in strict rotation, to resume for ten days each, a measure of the connubial bliss which had so long been denied them. John Cooper had put the idea to me before we left Dhofar and, at a farewell audience of the Sultan, I had bravely asked for his permission for wives to visit. This was unheard of; European ladies were only allowed into the Sultanate if accompanying their resident and very senior husbands.

"Where would they live?" asked his Highness.

"In my bungalow, while I am on leave, Sir."

"Would they be kept away from the town and the soldiers?"

"They would conform with any instructions you wish to impose."

"All right. Tell Brigadier Waterfield."

I told Brigadier Waterfield with the greatest pleasure: Pat Waterfield, the Military Secretary, an Olympian figure to whom everything had to be referred, whether it be the mode of dress for ladies attending the Queen's birthday party at the Consulate or an order to purchase a new Bren gun.

He smiled tolerantly when I told him of my plan.

"The Sultan will never allow it," he said. "No European woman has ever been allowed into the interior. Even my own wife isn't allowed in." A charming smile with a shake of the head.

"But I spoke to the Sultan before I left for Dhofar. He's agreed."

The Military Secretary accepted defeat gracefully. He smiled doubtfully.

"Oh, all right. If he says so. But mind they behave themselves."

So the wives came. And behaved themselves. And in due course, nine months to be precise, I acquired two additional godchildren. The other couple got divorced.

The battalion's deployment in Northern Oman was a legacy from the Jebel War of 1957, when the Imam, Ghalib bin Ali al Hini, and his brother Talib, supported by Saudi Arabia, rebelled against the Sultan, rallied the tribes of the Interior to their cause and waged a fierce guerrilla war against the inadequate Sultan's Armed Forces. Despite Arab League opposition, Sultan Said appealed to Britain for aid and reinforcements from the Cameronians, Trucial Oman Scouts, the Life Guards and finally the SAS, together with the reorganized SAF under Colonel David Smiley, combined to drive the rebels into the lofty fort of the Jebel Akhdar, from which they were ultimately dislodged. (John Cooper had commanded an SAS squadron in that battle and told many a tale of heroism and prodigious physical effort on that cruelly magnificent mountain.)

Thus the present day SAF was disposed throughout Northern Oman in the camps and villages which surrounded the Jebel Akhdar and whose approaches they dominated. Bid Bid, the gateway to the interior, where the shoulders of the Hajar Mountains overlooked the sparkling wadi and single track ford at Fanjah; Izki, a troublesome village to the south-west and Rostaq, with its massive fort, the ancient capital of the interior and citadel of the north-eastern approaches to the Green Mountain. Further west, another battalion, the Northern Frontier Regiment, occupied Nizwa, the ancient seat of the Imam of Oman, Balad Sait Ibri, on the Northern Border and that refuge of the rebels eight thousand feet up the mountain, the terraced village of Saiq.

These erstwhile trouble spots we patrolled regularly, to remind the village elders of their loyalty to the Sultan and of the omnipresence of his troops, to pay respects to the Walis and to assist the people in their still primitive living. Their needs were many: perhaps for water or medical aid, for communications or transport, for there was no civil administration and the villagers scratched the barest existence from their date palms, meagre crops and flocks of goats, while their children grew up with runny noses and fly-blown eyes which too often softened into the milk-white opacity of trachoma.

The Commander of the Sultan's Armed Forces, Brigadier Corran Purdon, was a delightful Ulsterman who had won an MC as a nineteen-year old Commander in the St Nazaire raid of 1940 and spent the rest of the war in Colditz. He was a gifted and popular commander and an energetic trainer of men. Soon after our return to the north he directed me to lay on a presentation for all the officers of the Force, based on our recent tour in Dhofar. We planned a series of lecture/presentations on actual operations, with the officers, NCOs and men who had taken part doing the talking, each part carefully rehearsed to bring out certain lessons, (we emphasized the mistakes as well as the successes) and supported by films and slides of the terrain and battle locations. I was anxious to include the whole range of options available to a commander there and thus described the smallest operation as well as the largest, involving the whole battalion with aircraft in support, as in the opening chapter. Jules Brett, the laconic but highly professional pilot who had commanded the aircraft that day, was a modest reminder of the hazards involved in air support; I remembered all too vividly seeing his Provost streaming smoke and the horror of seeing another supporting aircraft diving, guns spitting on to my own C Company. However, the presentation was fun to do and useful to the staff and units who had not yet served in the south.

Meanwhile, in Dhofar, the Desert Regiment (DR), newly formed, under strength and still not fully trained, was experiencing a whole new situation in the campaign, which had changed in the enemy's favour. British forces had started to withdraw from bases in the East Aden Protectorate in August, 1967, and by the end of November had begun to pull out of Aden itself. The socialist revolution which followed the rather tenuous assumption of power by the NLF had an immediate effect on the Dhofar rebellion and the committed Marxist-Leninists in Aden began to supply bases, equipment, training and direction to the DLF. The British had handed over large stocks of infantry weapons and ammunition, including mines, to the Federal Regular Army and these were quickly diverted to the Comrades in Dhofar.

One of Sultan Said's rather obstinate diversions from the main military effort was to build a fort on the Western Dhofar border with the East Aden Protectorate (now called the Peoples' Democratic Republic of South Yemen or PDRY). This was of no military significance whatever; it merely compensated for and was geographically opposite an almost identical and meaningless symbol built by the South Yemenis across the wadi. The Sultan's workmen did, however, require constant protection and all the materials for its construction had to be flown in by air. It thus dictated a prolonged and considerable diversion of already inadequate land and air forces at a critical time. The DLF took fresh heart.

In December, 1967, the rebels received much-needed supplies from the small desert seaport of Hawf in South Yemen, just across the border. Within days, a company of DR was engaged by forty DLF east of the Midway road and lost five killed and seven wounded. Enemy casualties were higher, but it was a measure of a new confidence that battle was joined on such a scale. Following this were incidents of mined vehicles and DR positions being attacked with mortars and machine guns. At the same time Intelligence reports confirmed that the DLF was becoming increasingly politicized. Aid from communist régimes was pouring in through PDRY. China provided arms, ammunition and military advisers and trained thirty members of the DLF as military leaders and political commissars at the Anti-Imperialist School in Peking.

In the north there was much to be done before we ourselves again became due for another year's tour of operations in Dhofar. We settled down to a steady and prolonged period of training. Although the great majority of the soldiers were long-service volunteers from both Oman and Baluchistan, many experienced officers, NCOs and men had left the battalion on posting or for civilian life. New recruits arrived. Of the British officers, one company commander, the experienced Peter Raven, left, as did the Marine Commando, Mark Murray, and two of my younger and more amusing officers, Nick Roberts and Toney Carey. They were replaced by Guy Sheridan, David Bayley, Patrick Brooke and Ranulph Twistleton-Wykeham-Fiennes. Guy Sheridan was another Marine, whose father I had known in Malaya. Guy was an Olympic langlauf skier and trained for this event by running along the seashore on skis. Patrick Brook and Ranulph Fiennes were both cavalrymen, a background about which CSAF had reservations.

"All these cavalrymen, Peter," he said, "They're good chaps, but this is an infantryman's war."

"Don't worry, sir, send them all to me. They're much quicker on the wireless set and usually less boring than heavy infantry."

And so they proved to be. The endless intercommunication between tanks on training exercises in Germany brought a snap and precision to our habitually cumbersome battalion command net and speeded up operations appreciably. In my two and a half years' command of this infantry battalion, I had five officers from the Royal Marines and seven from the cavalry and there wasn't a dud among them. Of the Marines, every one was decorated for gallantry.

I later took on Peter Bennett and Richard Kinsella-Bevan, both cavalrymen, Peter an ex-12th Lancer and SAS, Richard an Inniskilling Dragoon.

Ranulph Fiennes had had a chequered career. Tiring of successive years with the Greys on training in Germany, he had volunteered for SAS training, passed all the vigorous and inhuman trials to which they subject their volunteers and, just after final acceptance, had conceived the idea of blowing up the film set of *Doctor Dolittle* in Castle Combe. Ranulph and a few friends were convinced that the film company were desecrating the most beautiful village in England against its collective will and decided on a demonstration against this ruthless commercialism. In fact, the gentle villagers of Castle Combe were rather displeased with this righteous explosion since they were doing quite nicely out of the deal. Ranulph was convicted, fined heavily and told he was no longer considered suitable for 22 SAS.

Patrick Brook was a Blues and Royals officer who quickly proved his worth and had an uncanny knack of inventing nicknames for everyone, which stuck. He was soon to be the first of us to bump the enemy on our next tour in Dhofar when he was shot through the shoulder.

David Bayley had done National Service in the Rifle Brigade and the Royal Sussex Regiment and subsequently served in the esoteric and irregular band of officers, mostly SAS, who fought for the Yemeni Royalists in a bitter but ultimately unsuccessful guerrilla campaign against Nasser's Egyptians in 1964-66.

Simon, my Adjutant, took over command of C Company. There were thus several new officers of varying background and experience to train in those techniques which were peculiar to the Dhofar campaign and the whole cycle of re-training — or upgrading — the ordinary soldier had to include all the specialist skills of mortar men, Vickers machine-gun crews, signallers, drivers and medical orderlies, as well as the basic skills of infantrymen.

One of the main problems to overcome was the traditional attitude of the Arab or Baluchi soldier towards fighting a war. For generations the accepted reaction of the tribesman to someone shooting at him was to get behind whatever cover was available (preferably a boulder but often a bush or tuft and bang away with his weapon in the general direction of the enemy, or, sometimes, according to taste, in the air, with his eyes tight shut. The idea of hawk-eyed marksmen engaging each other with deadly accuracy until one or other bit the sand was not widely accepted. Each side would engage each other for several hours quite happily, either until they ran out of ammunition or it got dark, after which they withdrew, honour having been satisfied. There was little desire to obtain a decision, one way or the other, in such an engagement and absolutely no inclination to close with the enemy. There were, of course, exceptions to this rule when, occasionally, a man's brother got hit or it had been a long day and he lost his temper and charged resolutely at the enemy, firing from the hip. But, by and large, one needed to impress upon all ranks the tactics of fire and movement, whereby one element of any force gave covering fire while another element would close on the enemy to kill, wound or capture him.

At Bid Bid, Rostaq and Izki we therefore embarked on a progressive programme of skill-at-arms, with the maximum of live firing on the range, field-firing exercises, battle inoculation, camouflage and fieldcraft, night patrolling and fire and all the mass of battle drills and techniques which must be carried out instinctively and often without orders when we returned to fight the guerrillas in Dhofar. I tried to improve every soldier's shooting while he himself was under fire. A series of targets at differing ranges would be put out against a natural stop butt of rock and wadi. The soldiers advanced towards them and would suddenly come under fire from securely hidden "enemy", who would fire live rounds over their heads.

Luckily, the first Battalion of my own regiment, the Grenadier Guards, was then stationed in Sharjah, a few hundred miles to the north, and its commander, David Hargreaves, an old friend, welcomed the opportunity to send down on attachment a strong team of officers and senior NCO instructors to assist in our training. The new British 81mm mortar was just coming into service to replace the 3-inch mortar and the Grenadiers gave us a useful conversion course. Our enemies in Dhofar had been using the 81mm, left behind in quantities when the British Forces had left Aden and it had been a matter for comment that the rebels outgunned us in range and accuracy — by courtesy of the British.

The Battalion was due to receive a number of awards for gallantry, resulting from our recent Dhofar tour and it seemed a good idea to stage a battalion drill parade at Bid Bid for the Brigadier to present them. Drill Sergeant Tom Day of the Grenadiers (I had first met him as a young Sergeant in Germany) and a team of five sergeant drill instructors set about improving the standard of drill and turnout of the Muscat Regiment and the old Grenadier custom of putting all officers in a squad with NCOs, to be chased about like recruits on the parade ground, proved hugely enjoyable for the

Arab soldiers. It was the first time a whole battalion of SAF had paraded for many years and it was a great success. Arab soldiers responded enthusiastically to good instructions at drill; they are immensely proud of their appearance and bearing and happily spend hours polishing their weapons and equipment.

The routine was pleasantly purposeful without being frenetic; reveille at 5.30 am in order to get most of the serious training over before the weather was too hot. By midday the temperature rose to 120 degrees F in the shade, the sun warming the volcanic rock and shale so that the heat burned through the sole of our boots, but the first hours after dawn were cool and crystal clear and we had three hours of energetic action before the haze made rifle shooting impossible and the sun's heat addled the brain.

At nine we had long leisurely breakfasts with three-day-old newspapers. Huge quantities of fresh fishcakes and monumental fry-ups were washed down with pints of loomi (fresh lime juice, sugar and water) or tinned orange juice. Then, out on the range again, or to a neighbouring wadi, or to the office, until two pm, a light lunch, a sleep and back to the office from five to seven.

The situation in Dhofar demanded that the battalion there should be permanently reinforced by an additional company, loaned in turn by each battalion in the north. The Force Commander warned me in May that year, 1968, that we were to provide a company to come under command of the Northern Frontier Regiment and I decided to send Richard John's A Company since Richard was the only company commander with Dhofar experience. Since returning from Dhofar in November they had been stationed at Rostaq, the picturesque former capital of the Interior which, with its rambling, magnificent fort guarded the north-eastern approaches to the Jebel Akhdar.

Thither I went by Landrover, across the flat, stony Batinah Plain, running broadly parallel to the coast, then turning inland towards the mountains. Richard had arranged a *Fadl*[17] for all ranks and we sat on the cement floor of one of the barrack huts, covered with army blankets, while huge flat dishes were placed before each group, on which were piled mounds of rice, spotted with sultanas and surrounded by hunks of freshly killed goat. These were torn apart by the hosts (the assembled soldiery), handed to you and eaten meticulously in the right hand. I never liked the tasteless, rather

71

stringy texture of goat meat and in some seven years of Arabia I never learned to squeeze the fat out or the rice and mould it into a ball without burning both hand and lips and scattering grains of rice over myself and my neighbours. The second course was invariably tinned peaches or pineapple, equally difficult to eat elegantly with the fingers. And then the soldiers, miraculously merry — for all this was washed down with tepid water and weak coffee — would start to sing. They sang haunting, rather monotonous songs, which gradually changed to rhythmic chants with ribald lyrics. Ultimately, someone got up to dance and, understandably in this all-male environment, the dancer would impersonate a female.

Corporal Issa Shetait was the star. With a flamboyant pair of scarlet underpants over his army trousers and a strip of coloured cloth for a bra over his shirt, he gave a masterly striptease, wriggling his hips and undulating his belly as the onlookers responded with ever more lewd gestures and bawdy cries.

Suddenly it was all over and we drifted away to bed in a haze of camaraderie and cigarette smoke. Every soldier shook hands with Richard and myself before leaving. I sent C Company, under Simon over to Rostaq from Bid Bid and Richard set off for the long journey south.

Meanwhile, in the south, the Desert Regiment had been relieved by Mike Harvey's Northern Frontier Regiment. Mike Harvey had won an MC on the Imjin River in Korea, leading out the remnants of the Gloucestershire Regiment from encircling Chinese hordes. Surrounded, he had taken the bold decision to go north, deeper into the Chinese-held territory, rather than directly towards his own lines. He had then circled west and south and into the American lines, entering which he had been shot up by American Sherman tanks. Mike was a tough, remorseless officer and a fitness fanatic, widely experienced in both conventional war and the counter-guerrilla operations which sometimes pass for peace. Mike hated Communism with a calculating, dedicated hatred and he knew *The Thoughts of Chairman Mao* by heart. He had trained his battalion to the nth degree and it had already achieved spectacular results in Dhofar against the gradually reinforced rebels.

There was evidence that the structure of the opposition had changed significantly; Salim bin Nufl, the father of the original rebellion, wounded in 1966, had taken refuge in Saudi Arabia. In the face of significant tribal factions within the DLF, he had admitted that his revolution was purely Nationalist and had refused to accept overt aid from Communist sources. He had even said that he would be willing to accept the Sultan as ruler, if he, bin Nufl and his group, were allowed back into Dhofar to take part in the Government. But this was not all in accord with the Qarra faction of the movement, traditionally opposed to bin Nufl's tribe of the Bait Kathiri. The Qarra leaders were backed and trained by the Chinese and, increasingly, by the Russians, and it was their aim to purge the guerrilla movement of all nationalist and radical Muslims — indeed of anyone who was not totally committed to the Marxist class struggle.

The Northern Frontier Regiment, in their frequent contacts in Dhofar, had killed or captured guerrillas with *The Thoughts of Chairman Mao* in their tunic pockets, each rebel armed with an automatic Kalashnikov rifle. This clear evidence of Marxist indoctrination of, and participation in, the opposition came as a relief to most of the British personnel serving in the Sultanate at this time. Many officers, myself included, welcomed Marxist intervention, with its naked policy of terrorism of the innocent, as balm to a troubled conscience. The nationalist rebels of the DLF had been ruthless and efficient killers, but we had seen with our own eyes how little had been done for their people. While the Sultan's resources were so pitifully inadequate, this was understandable, but with the beginning of oil revenues in 1967 there was surely something that could be done to relieve the terrible toll of hunger and disease which afflicted the Dhofaris. Was there not a suspicion that we, the British, were lending support to a corrupt regime, whereby the Sultan, so amiable and paternal, and his chosen few, lived in comfort and careless ignorance, while the great mass of people barely scratched an existence from their starving herds, their children growing precariously in a world of disease and squalor, with no hope of human progress towards greater knowledge, health or experience.

But with Marxism we knew we were helping to combat a known evil. Already there were stories of terrible intimidation and torture among the tribes on the Jebel; of uncooperative tribesmen being burnt for refusing to offer up their meat or milk or money to the local commissars. The voice of Cairo and Aden radio beamed the familiar drivel throughout the Sultanate at every hour of the day.

"Throw off the harness of British Imperialism. Take the wealth that is yours but is stolen by the Sultan. Why does he hide from you amongst his harem in distant Dhofar?"

This familiar, repeated evidence of a more ruthless and menacing regime at work both salved our conscience and gave us a whole new purpose to the campaign.

7

Like Evelyn Waugh's Ben Ritchie-Hook, Mike Harvey and the NFR spent the latter half of 1968 dashing about Dhofar "biffing" the enemy. The DLF was becoming increasingly politicized. Aid from Communist régimes was flowing into Dhofar through PDRY.

Mike Harvey's well-trained battalion had marked success under his virulently anti-Communist leadership. He maintained the overall strategic aim which had been established before I arrived, of operating on the routes into the Jebel from the west, where enemy movement would be canalized, but he wisely moved further west, into the Wadi Sayq area and eventually established a company base at Defa a few miles west of our old base at Janook, and better placed to patrol against the cavernous Wadi Sayq, which already showed signs of containing a large enemy base.

In May, Richard John, operating under command of NFR in the Wadi Hinna, was severely wounded in the chest and shoulder. Corporal Issa Shetait, beside him, was killed outright. Richard was evacuated on a donkey to the nearest level ground where a Beaver could land. The journey took twelve hours; there was only enough morphia for three. The nearest available surgery was at the British Military Hospital in Bahrein, so after a rough dressing had been put on by the NFR medical officer, Richard was loaded on to an RAF plane and finally received the first necessary surgery some 900 miles and 36 hours after being wounded. The shortcomings of SAF administration were again frighteningly demonstrated. Issa Shetait was buried in the gradually expanding burial plot for Muslims a few hundred yards from Umm al Ghawarif camp. As I wrote a letter of commiseration to his wife I remembered his light-hearted dancing girl of a few weeks before, at Rostaq: "He was loved and respected...died gallantly doing his duty." But I knew his wife could not possibly understand the meaning of his death, six hundred miles away in a wild country she had never seen, against an enemy with whom she had no quarrel.

A month later, in the same Wadi Hinna, C Company, commanded by Tim Landon, on loan to NFR, responded by killing three enemy and capturing four, urged on by an enthusiastic Corran Purdon who went along for the ride.

One was wearing Chinese insignia, finally providing firm evidence of rebel Chinese involvement. This change from tribal rebellion to Communist revolution was formalized[18] at a Party Congress in the Wadi Hamrin. The newly-elected General Command of twenty-five included only three of the original 18-man DLF executive. The front was renamed The Popular Front for the Liberation of the Occupied Arabian Gulf (PFLOAG) with the aim of spreading organized armed struggle throughout the Gulf. The ideology was officially changed from nationalism to Marxism–Leninism and the revolutionary transformation of Dhofar planned. Political indoctrination of military cadres and the whole population went together with military training. Some rebels did not accept the changes and the Communists' method of ensuring compliance with the new order was brutal and effective. Dhofaris were tortured and executed in large numbers.

Mike Harvey's reaction to the increased Communist involvement was less ruthless but equally determined. He instituted a policy of blowing up or "capping" wells all over the Jebel which certainly inhibited enemy convoys but also denied water to the local and possibly innocent Jebalis and their herds. He detained and incarcerated a number of ancient Jebalis in the hope of successful interrogation and my officers were deeply sceptical of the reports of captured "PDRY soldiers".

I wasn't on the spot and couldn't judge, but it seemed to me that such action could only militate against the vital need to win — or at least not deliberately alienate — the hearts and minds of the people. Sultan Said warmly approved oppressive action against the Jebalis. His philosophy was "those that are not with me are against me" and he found a loyal servant of his policy in Mike Harvey. This contrasted sharply with the standard British Army policy of trying to separate the neutral sheep from the committed Marxist goats, to support and protect the former and harass and destroy the latter.

Corran Purdon, meanwhile, supported all his battalion commanders by frequent visits to Dhofar, determined to take part in as many operations as possible, and used his knowledge of our difficulties to back his continual requests to the Sultan for the urgent provision of helicopters, the formation of a fourth infantry battalion, for efforts to win the hearts and minds of the Dhofaris and for the secondment from Britain of the SAS. All, at that time, to no avail.

Lieutenant-Colonel John Slim, commanding 22 SAS, arrived with little warning, at my Mess at Bid Bid. After he had drunk a certain amount of Bacardi rum and loomi, I asked him what was behind his visit, although I suspected I knew.

"Trying to find a job for my boys," said John.

Since the end of the Borneo campaign and the evacuation from Aden, 22 SAS had been unable to find an operational role and Dhofar was the obvious answer for their special skills. John regaled us with tales of his intrepid men on recent exercises off the coast of Sharjah, "wading ashore through shark-infested waters and operating in desert for thirty-six hours without water." This was greeted by fairly hollow laughter by my assembled officers, at least four of whom were ex-SAS and most of whom had just completed a year on operations against a live enemy, severely restricted by rationed water — and who now spent most of their weekend swimming in shark-infested water, for fun, off the sandy beaches of Mina al Fahal.

None of us needed convincing of the quality and professionalism of 22 SAS and we all hoped that John would be successful in helping to convince the British Government to deploy them in Dhofar. However, the political climate was not right. Mr. Wilson's Government, in the midst of a general scuttle from Aden and the Gulf, could not then countenance formed British units (as opposed to individuals on loan) being deployed to assist a reactionary and autocratic potentate, however pro-Western his views.

It was not until September, 1970, that their attitude changed and the first group of SAS arrived to start the hugely successful hearts and minds campaign which, combined with increased military pressure over a further five years, was to win the war.

John Slim good-naturedly took a lot of ribbing from the former SAS officers in my Regiment and also Simon, whose father had commanded the SAS and had John as his adjutant. Spotting Ranulph Fiennes in the Mess, John Slim told an intriguing story, albeit against himself. When Ranulph, a relaxed, even suspect, Cavalry officer, had been undergoing training for 22 SAS, John, as Commanding Officer, had noticed him apparently asleep on the back of the class. When the Colonel had prodded him awake and given him a rocket, Ranulph protested, "But I have been paying attention, Colonel," and immediately summarized every point the lecturer had covered without fault.

Brigadier Corran Purdon very sensibly decreed that all officers joining the Force should go down to Dhofar to be attached to the Regiment on operations, and learn something of the conditions there, before going into action with their own regiments. He even extended this ruling to his own staff and every officer in the Force Services — Ordnance, EME, Supply and so on — so that every headquarters or "base" officer had practical and recent experience of operations on the Jebel. This increased their appreciation of problems at the sharp end and entirely eliminated that resentment which sometimes exists between front line units and the staff.

Thus, in August of that year David Bayley and Ranulph Fiennes, newly arrived at Bid Bid, went down to Dhofar on attachment to NFR to learn all they could about the increasingly active guerrilla campaign which was developing. The south-east monsoon started towards the end of July and in the dense, protective mist which enveloped the Jebel and its approaches the rebels had become increasingly daring in attacking SAF on the Salalah Plain, an entirely new development since we were last in Dhofar.

David and Ranulph, attached to B Company NFR, were quickly involved in a typical "contact" in the foothills leading up to the escarpment. Mike Harvey's "Emergency Regulations, Dhofar" stipulated that all travellers from South Yemen would be directed back there by 26 October, after which the border would be closed. To enforce this with limited troops was of course impossible. Tracks, wells and passes on all routes from the west would be blown up and a curfew would be imposed throughout Dhofar after dark. Any armed person moving thereafter could be shot without first being challenged. Patrols were carried out on the edge of the plain, on which the Jebalis congregated during the monsoon, to collect wood, which they sold in Salalah. Mike's patrols ruthlessly removed all the males from these camps and took them back to Umm al Ghawarif camp to be interned for questioning. They might be imprisoned for days or weeks, on suspicion of helping the terrorists. While they were absent, many of their families came close to starvation. The aim was to gain intelligence of rebel movements and contacts and to persuade the local people to refuse aid to the guerrillas. Ranulph became convinced that neither purpose was being achieved and that, if anything, those tribesmen as yet uncommitted were being driven to hate the Army and the Sultan we served.

Inevitably, the plain patrols drew the attention of the enemy. Ranulph and David received their baptism of fire attached to the experienced Bill Prince's company. Leaving their lorries well back on the plain they marched by night into the foothills, cursing their way through the sharp thorn bushes which tore at their clothes and flesh. They lay up in the damp mist of the Khareef, sweaty from the long march, their clothes suddenly cold and clinging in the long wait until dawn.

At first light they rose to cordon and search a kraal-like village and almost immediately came under fire from the departing rebels. Among the meat and entrails of a freshly-butchered goat close by the huts lay some spent .303 cartridges in the mud — the sign that only locally recruited militia had been about, not the fully-fledged guerrillas who were armed with AK47 Kalashnikov automatic rifles.

The guerrillas had gone, melting through the mist and the cordon still being adjusted round the village in the dark. But the adoo were gradually growing stronger and more daring in their attacks. A few days later RAF Salalah was mortared for the first time. The bombs had done no damage and the expected follow-up attacks had not materialized, but to get their mortars within range the rebels had marched, carrying the component parts of the mortar separately — heavy base plate, barrel and bipod — across five miles of open plain, at great risk to their subsequent withdrawal. SAF troops following up the next morning could find no trace of the base plate position. Empty rounds, packing, fuse-caps had all been carried away or buried in the sand for a future occasion.

The next day the sewage disposal lorries from RAF Salalah were shot up by the rebels. The Pakistani drivers routinely drove their lorries across the flat gravel plain north of Salalah, using the same tracks on each occasion, to dump camp refuse among the foothills beneath the escarpment. Guerrillas seize upon anyone who establishes a set pattern and the timing and route of the sewage lorries had been marked by the adoo over a long period.

The first burst of automatic fire brought the leading vehicle to a halt and produced a column of black smoke from its engine. The second burst smashed into the driver's legs, five or six bullets shattering the tibula and fibula into a bloody mess. Somehow, the second driver bravely manhandled his mate out of the wrecked vehicle and into his own. Luckily, the adoo, well-satisfied, failed to follow up the attack and the undamaged lorry returned to camp.

The adoo did, however, wait for the inevitable follow up by the soldiers from Umm al Ghawarif camp, and when Ranulph arrived with his two platoons of Bill Prince's company he advanced under cover of the company's 81mm mortars towards the burnt-out truck. They did so routinely, almost casually, thinking of breakfast, for the Adoo had never, hitherto, stayed on the plain by daylight for fear of the Provost fighters of the Sultan's Air Force. Ranulph and B Company were rudely disillusioned when they suddenly came under heavy automatic fire barely three hundred yards from the ant hills which concealed some fifty adoo in well-prepared sangars.

They were lucky. There is a tendency for inexperienced marksmen to aim high and these adoo were still perhaps getting accustomed to the new Kalashnikov rifles. The NFR platoons were caught in the open without a scrap of cover but the bullets cracked overhead and winged away harmlessly. Gallantly, the Staff Sergeant on Ranulph's right charged straight for the enemy while Ranulph organized the other platoon to give covering fire. Then they too clambered to their feet to close up on the Staff Sergeant in another tactical bound. Again the Staff Sergeant charged with his men but now the distance was closer and the next adoo burst bowled him over, his rifle flying from outstretched arms, and he lay still.

Then the first mortar bombs, fired by the watchful Bill Prince, started bursting among the ant hills. Soon the lone Provost fighter dived on the enemy positions and dropped 250lb fragmentation bombs. Don Angus, a laconic Scot flying the Provost, climbed out of his bombing run and turned into another dive. High above the scream of the engine and his rabid covering fire, Ranulph could see a stream of enemy tracer strike the little plane. One burst jammed the controls so that the plane climbed vertically and hung in the air, as if about to stall. Angus, out of control, slid his cockpit cover back and prepared to jump. Suddenly the joystick unjammed and he recovered control and flew the plane back to Salalah, a few miles away.

The guerrillas withdrew. As always, they preferred not to hang around when SAF closed in in greater strength. Bill Prince's company found empty machine-gun clips and cases and bloodstained rags, but no bodies. A few days later Radio Aden claimed that the glorious freedom fighters of Dhofar had suffered six dead and ten wounded but "had destroyed a Hawker Hunter and killed forty-nine of the British Imperialist troops".

Back in Bid Bid we were kept informed, either by directives from HQ SAF or by the gripping tales of officers passing through, of the development of operations in Dhofar and revised and adapted our training and organization accordingly. Mike Harvey reckoned the average strength of enemy groups was now greater and with greater fire power than hitherto and in due course CSAF wisely issued a directive that SAF should never operate on the Jebel in less than half-company strength (about 50 men). The days were gone when lightly-equipped patrols of five or six men could venture on the Jebel unsupported. It was an ideal tactic but one that SAF could not use. We simply did not have enough soldiers of sufficient skill and experience. We did not have the communications nor the helicopters we would need. This ruling would mean that we would use up our limited troops in trying to cover all the tasks.

I therefore decided to build up the Recce Platoon from its usual 15-20 men to twice that size. Well-led and armed with automatic weapons, it could cover great distances in its Landrovers and give me the equivalent of an additional half-company to deploy. I also invited Ranulph, on his return from Dhofar, to concentrate on straightforward infantry training. All soldiers like swanning about vast tracts of desert in vehicles and Ranulph's Arabs had a smug superiority over their less fortunate brethren slogging through the desert on their feet. It was a fatal weakness in Dhofar to "motor into battle" when one well-aimed rocket launcher could write off a vehicle and five soldiers with one shot. Recently, four Landrovers of NFR had been trapped in a wadi and ambushed by three well-sited machine-gun groups. Two vehicles and their crews had been destroyed.

I wanted our Recce Platoon to be as good an independent half-company on their feet as any other and this was later proved to be a happy decision.

Unfortunately, I left Ranulph with instructions to build up his platoon to fifty, and then departed on leave to England to see my family and play a little polo. During my absence and armed with a letter from me authorizing him to cross-post five men from each company to his expanding platoon, Ranulph personally visited each company in turn, often when the company commander concerned was away. He interviewed the many applicants and departed with the cream of each company, leaving me to pacify the indignant company commanders on my return. I didn't know whether to applaud his initiative or censure his under-handedness, but the result, after some intensive training, was a very high calibre Recce Platoon, mostly Arab, and this was more appropriate to their independent role.

On my way back from leave I visited Richard John in the RAF hospital in Bahrein. He had been lucky, with some expert surgery and nursing, and although still in bed after numerous operations, was shortly due to go back to the rehabilitation centre at Headley Court for an agonizing programme of exercise and physiotherapy which would, I hoped, lead to a Medical Board passing him fit to return to the battalion for further duty. Bruce Hamilton, an old friend from the Staff College, and John Andrews, the Garrison Commander in Bahrein and their active and attractive wives, spoiled him rotten with visits and goodies while he was in hospital and did much to lessen his sense of isolation.

The tempo at Bid Bid was leisurely but purposeful. Gradually, the companies improved the standard of their shooting, section and platoon fieldcraft, personal and vehicle camouflage, physical fitness and all the hundred and one skills of the infantry soldier. New officers learned their trade by attachment to NFR in Dhofar — or rather, learned how little they knew and what they needed to learn. Gradually we progressed to battalion level training, starting with headquarters signal exercises, in which battalion headquarters and

9. The arrival of a land convoy at Midway after a 600-mile drive across the desert from the North.

10. The relative tranquility of the North; Rostaq's majestic Portugese fort.

11. A Beaver resupply plane landing at Rostaq.

12. 81mm mortar-engaging targets on the far side of the Wadi Jardoom.

13. Opening up the Midway Road — a temporary lull.

14. Guy Sheridan checking out DF tasks.

15. Peter Thwaites (at the wheel) arriving at Raven's Roost.

16. Officers' Mess at Raven's Roost — Peter Bennett, Guy Sheridan and Simon Sloane.

each company practised themselves and their wireless operators in rapid communication with each other and with supporting elements like mortars, machine guns, artillery and the Air Force. I was well-pleased, and faintly surprised, when all this came together in a final signals exercise on the Batinah, with the whole vital rigmarole of reporting locations, correctly encoded, indicating targets, relating positions on the ground to an inadequate map and was rapidly achieved over wide distances, with the minimum of technical problems and every station coming up loud and clear in sequence. The cavalry officer's crisp, staccato "One — OK — out!" was in marked contrast to the mournful litany of the infantry: "Hallo,won,Hallo,won — How do you hear me? Won, nothing heard. OUT" Pack up, close down, kip down.

There was one serious defect in SAF's communication procedure. The Air Ministry refused to allow SOAF to teach even basic training in Arabic. While every regular Army officer on secondment to SAF had to attend an extensive Arabic course before starting his tour, the Air Ministry, remarkably, didn't consider it necessary. Not only did this prohibit officers of the Sultan's Air Force from extending the simplest courtesies in their own language to Arab colleagues, it was operationally inefficient and occasionally disastrous. There were many occasions when a body of ground troops, in contact with the enemy, would not have a British officer within reach to direct aircraft's supporting fire. Platoons were commanded by Arab or Baluchi Staff Sergeants who spoke no English and who, whilst in good wireless contact with an aircraft overhead, could not make themselves understood to the pilot to give vital target indication. The RAF made no attempt to give their pilots even the simplest understanding of instructions in Arabic and, curiously enough, I never knew a pilot who tried to learn. A timely direction to "Go north 200 yards" in Arabic should not have been difficult to learn and would quite possibly mean the difference between life and death.

Each company commander was aware of the need to have a highly operational, efficient and motivated force by the time we went down to Dhofar — if only for self-preservation. Simon Sloane, commanding C Company at Rostaq, marched his company to the top of the Jebel Akhdar for a three-day exercise, and I went with them. The northern face of the mountain was the shortest but also the steepest approach. Leaving the vehicles on the floor of the narrow Wadi Awabi, we started climbing, with the support weapons, water and rations for three days on donkeys. The way was precipitous, strewn with huge boulders, in many of which rough steps had been cut, or worn away by the footsteps of a thousand years. Until midday we made good progress shaded from the sun by the massif of the mountain itself. Later, we took frequent halts, practising the strictest water discipline and I was amazed how fit the soldiers were and how agile the donkeys and their handlers. In spite of the fierce heat of the sun reflecting off the rocks, the soldiers seemed to have no difficulty in saving the water in their bottles. I found thirst the most painful part of the exercise.

After some eight hours' climb the rocky path opened onto a long sloping plateau with a sprinkling of small green bushes and rocky outcrops, not unlike Dhofar, but less rugged. Here the company bivouacked to carry out its training and I started down the mountain alone. It was now the hottest part of the day and I had rather overestimated my powers of strength. Going down was more tiring than going up and the strain on the knee joints was acute. Soon after leaving the summit I turned my ankle over, jumping from one great grey slab to another. My whole weight fell on it and I thought it might be broken. I continued the descent on all fours which was effective but slow. After a few hours of some discomfort, I was met by two of the donkey handlers from the rear party in the wadi bed. They had observed from several thousand feet below my peculiar manner of descent and come to my rescue with "Breakdown", one of the biggest and strongest of the donkeys, who frequently towed the others. I mounted "Breakdown" gratefully and arrived at the bottom in one piece and great pain.

The incident gave me pause to reflect, however. On such a march in Dhofar, I would have been a handicap to any body of marching troops. I was forty-one years old, probably the oldest man in the battalion and with only one moderately efficient kidney. I must gauge my performance on operations carefully.

Meanwhile, the efforts of Pat Waterfield and Corran Purdon to update much of the old-fashioned SAF weaponry bore fruit.

The new British self-loading rifle, the FN *(Fabrique Nationale)* arrived in batches and each company converted to it in turn, gladly handing in the old bolt-action No.4 rifles, which had not significantly changed in design since 1914 — and the soldiers were delighted that they could now compete on level terms with the enemy Kalashnikovs. With the new rifles came the GPMG, a heavy machine gun, but we were allowed to keep the old Vickers Medium Machine Gun which served us so well and thereby further increased our fire-power. Best of all, the heavy and cumbersome 19 and BCC 30 wireless sets were replaced by a wonderful new range of Racal sets, the best of which gave flawless voice communication over some thirty miles of mountainous terrain and could be lifted on to a man's back with one hand. All these items were received like manna from heaven by the soldiers who set to learning how to operate and maintain them with child-like enthusiasm.

Finally, we rehearsed the whole orchestra — of men, weapons, equipment and machines — in a glorious exercise involving battalion headquarters, all three rifle companies, support weapons, administrative elements and the Air Force in a wide wadi about thirty miles from Bid Bid. The dreaded Recce Platoon acted as enemy and were told to be as daring and aggressive as the real rebels in Dhofar. They took this very seriously; they ambushed us before the exercise officially started, threw stones at us when we assaulted their position and blew up blanks and explosive charges in our faces. When night fell and we were securely in our hastily-built sangars, they attacked us with fiendish stealth and ingenuity with an overwhelming weight of blank ammunition and pyrotechnics until, as I rallied my men and told them to sit tight in their position, the unmistakable 'crack-thump-peeooo!' of a live round whizzed past my ear. This could be dangerous, I thought, and blew the whistle. Whether it was a genuine mistake, whereby a live round got mixed up with the blanks, or an over-zealous member of the Recce Platoon determined to "win" I never discovered. Apart from this premature end to the night attack the exercise was a success and everything went well.

In the midst of this practice and preparation for war there were interludes, like patches of shade in the white hot sunlight, of almost idyllic peace. My mother's sister, Aunt Joan Forsyth, aged eighty-two, flew from America to visit me. Kind friends smoothed her path. Christopher Thursby-Pelham, Chief of Staff in Bahrein, whisked her from the airport to his house and delivered her back the following morning to catch the Fokker Friendship to Muscat.

Corran and Patricia Purdon kindly welcomed her for another night's rest at their attractive bungalow at Bait al Falaj from which I collected her the following morning, to whisk her, wrapped like a Bedu in the open Landrover, up the red laterite road to Bid Bid. She stayed in my spare room, emerging indomitably for day trips to Fanjah, Nizwa and the exquisite Wadi Sumail. This was the old route from Muscat to the Interior, its chequered history of tribal feud and massacre reflected in the sparkling pools of the wadi and the long line of forts and watch-towers scattered along its entire length. Here we visited Khamis bin Humaid, the charming "*siyassi*"[19] who gave us coffee and dates and halwa on his rooftop, surrounded by the oranges, limes, pomegranates and small seedless grapes which grew all along the wadi.

To Izki, where David Bayley entertained us in his mess and on to Nizwa, on rough, graded road, to the ancient capital of the Interior. Few European women were allowed into the Interior, so I did not make my usual courtesy call on the Wali. However, he kindly allowed us into the great mediaeval fort where we viewed the emblazoned canon, captured from the Portuguese in the sixteenth century, and the foul-smelling oubliette, where prisoners rotted less than fifty years ago.

The fort still served as the city's jail and today's prisoners, shuffling past in heavy leg-irons, greeted us cheerfully and shook hands. One, a boy of perhaps eight or nine with laughing eyes and a dirty face, was doing time for throwing stones at the Wali.

The suq at Nizwa was famed for its silverware and for centuries the Bedouin had been forced to realize the capital their heirlooms represented. Wide, heavily embossed silver anklets and bracelets, delicate necklaces, finger and toe rings gleamed dully in cardboard boxes. Nearby, a patrician old man with a long white beard hammered away at his trade. He was known as Ali bin Coffee Pot. A few months earlier I had given him a bag of Maria Theresa dollars, half of which he melted down to make an exquisite traditional Omani coffee pot and half of which he kept for his labour. I have it still, the silver delicately engraved, the spout curved like the beak of a bird of prey.

We sallied to Muscat some two hours down the dirt road, through the foothills of the Hajar Mountains, across the Batinah Plain, up and over the sudden sharp barrier of jagged volcanic rock, which shielded from all sides but the sea the walled city of Muscat. As we motored up the narrow winding road, gravelly and ungraded, with its precipitous Z bends, the wheels of the sturdiest Landrover scrabbled and slipped and the furnace heat of the sun was reflected off the jagged rocks, doubling the normal air temperature. "The heat of Muscat is a glimpse of eternity," wrote some 11th century explorer but viewed from the top of the pass in neat panorama, the town looked cool and inviting. Height and distance lent enchantment to the square, white houses, slim minarets and winding streets and, dominating all, the twin grey forts of Jelali and Murani, flanking the entrance to the crescent blue of Muscat harbour.

This bewitching view, so often the visitor's first sight of Muscat, concealed the squalid reality of closer inspection, of open drains, of rotting fish and the sickly smell of human ordure along the sea-shore.

We entered through the Bab el Kabir (the big gate) in the city wall which followed the line of rocky peaks from the sea on each side of the city, each peak topped by a watch-tower. Richard Anderson, the portly Garrison Commander, suspended his noted misogyny and courteously showed my aunt round the ancient arsenal in Fort Murani, over which he presided. Named after a 16th century sea captain of the Portuguese occupation, it dominated the entrance to the little harbour, with a fine view of the great rock on which successive visiting crews had carved the names of their ship — what the Sultan called his "visiting book". Here a young Nelson was alleged to have climbed the sheer rock-face to write *Euryalus* on the topmost peak. Here, in a later war, a Japanese midget submarine had penetrated, submerged, through the tiny gap between the two rocks to blow an Allied merchantman out of the water and retire undetected.

Richard gave us great draughts of loomi before we departed for the suq, where the smell of spices, fresh fruit and fish did much to dispel the stench which pervaded the twisting alleyways.

In the gold market craftsmen wrought delicate filigree brooches and necklaces from 10-Tolar bars, heating and hammering the metal in the suffocating air temperature. We called on Bill Carden in the white stone Consulate, its massive walls softened by latticed balconies overlooking the granite crags and blue water of Muscat

Bay.

Bill was a kind, wise man, but I was struck by the fundamental difference of approach in our views. He had once shown me a paper by him or one of his staff on the situation in the Sultanate, which would go to the Foreign Office. In meticulous detail and matchless prose it outlined the historical background, the economic consequences of future oil revenues, the character of the Sultan, the unrest in Dhofar, the dangers of a take-over from South Yemen, supported by China, the fertile soil for the weeds of Marxism in the deprived and backward people — every relevant factor was mentioned, discussed and observed upon, dissected, the possible outcome of each option (where there was an option) or eventuality meticulously weighed in the balance. "On the one hand...but it must be borne in mind that...on the other hand...". Then the paper ended.

"What do you think of it?" said Bill. "I think it's rather good."

"It's lovely," I said light-heartedly. "Articulate, comprehensive, scholarly; but where's the end?"

"It's there. That's it." said Bill.

"Oh, dear," I said. "Now, to us stupid soldiers, that paper is quite valueless. We are taught that no paper is of any use to anyone unless it not only outlines and discusses the pros and cons, but also makes a clear recommendation for action. Anyone reading this paper will be impressed by its evaluation of all the factors but still won't have the faintest idea of what to do about them!"

"Ah," said Bill. "That's what we in the Foreign Office aim at. The diplomat must take account of all the relevant factors, weigh up all the pros and cons, outline the possible options and their likely effect, but he must never, on any account, come to any conclusion and never make a recommendation. He might be wrong."

I drove to Izki to visit Peter Raven's company. At lunch in the little garden he had nurtured from the sand around the Officers' Mess, there were two American oil men — pipeliners — laying the massive ducts from Fahud, the oilfields in the dunes south of Nizwa, to the harbour terminal near Muscat at Mina al Fahal. Chuck and Fred were tough guys, very professional and experienced, confident in a trade they had practised from the Gulf of Mexico to Alaska. They had called in for a break on the long journey from Muscat to the Interior. Their lunch was almost entirely liquid. They drank can after can of iced lager while we ate our sandwiches and gulped loomi. We tried to persuade them to sleep it off before continuing their journey in the cool of the evening but they laughed, loaded several crates of beer onto their Landrovers and departed in a cloud of dust.

An hour later, when I was finishing my inspection, one of the drivers reported the accident. The oil company's Landrover had left the road on a long, badly-graded bend some ten miles away and Chuck and Fred had been crushed.

The bodies were brought in. We searched their blood-soaked clothing for identification, found a few pathetic letters and snaps of wives and children and sent a wireless message to the oil company headquarters in Mina al Fahal.

"What are we going to do with the bodies? They won't last long in this heat."

I knew what was being suggested. I was bound for Bid Bid which was more than halfway back to Muscat. Clearly it was up to me. We piled them unceremoniously into the back of my Landrover and I drove off, asking that a message be sent to the oil company on the wireless.

The road was bumpy and dusty and the thud of those bodies on the floor of the vehicle is still clear in my memory. We arrived at the hospital long after dark and were directed to the mortuary. Here, I ran into trouble. Both Murad, my driver and the Pakistani night watchman were strict Muslims. Neither would touch a dead Nasrani. I had to manhandle the two heavy bodies myself.

As he surveyed the magnificence of the hospital I could almost read my Omani driver's thoughts. The oil company's camp, or colony, at Mina al Fahal was perched on the cliffs overlooking the sparkling sea, row upon row of neat bungalows each with neat gardens and trees lovingly tended by their European occupants, each house humming with air conditioners and glistening with the latest kitchen fittings, each garden sparkling with miraculous, unending water from a spout in the rocky sand; the hospital gleaming with chrome and tile, bed upon empty bed, operating theatre, X-ray and recreation rooms, pristine sheets awaiting Christmas patients — for there were few oil company casualties and no local Omani was admitted.

"*Sharika mumtaz!*"[20] said Murad in wonder. If the oil company money could produce these wonders for the Nasranis, interlopers in his own land, why could not more be done for the Omanis, (including his brother soldiers whom we had visited a few days ago) who were crammed, if they were lucky, into the tiny Mission hospital in Muttrah, where Doctor Wells Tomes and his wife coped valiantly with terrible disease and injury and goats roamed the wards because the visiting ladies could not leave them while the husbands were sick?

To me it seemed only a matter of time before every Omani became more aware of these inequalities and joined the revolt against an unfeeling Sultan. Change was inevitable. It must come either by revolution, which meant defeat of the present regime by the Marxist forces spreading north-eastwards from Dhofar, or by evolution, the peaceful victory by the Sultan over hearts and minds, through a fairer distribution of the resources rapidly becoming available.

8

Mike Harvey turned from the wall map. His eyes blinked mildly from behind thick glasses but he was as strong as an ox. His officers called him "Oddjob".

"Well, that's about it." He had given me an up-to-date briefing of his own dispositions which I was about to take over and areas of recent enemy activity. "We've had contacts here," he pointed at the map, "and here — and here. They use typical Marxist tactics now — 'Feint in the East — Strike in the West.' They're operating pretty well everywhere on the Jebel, but if you really want to bump them go West."

This certainly helped to clarify my intentions. Before leaving Bid Bid I had received a long directive from CSAF outlining his ideas on the operational situation in Dhofar and giving me his guidelines on how to conduct operations. The problem was that CSAF had pretty well hedged his bets. Unwilling perhaps to place an order of priority on the overall strategic — or complementary tactical — objectives, he had set down a confusing and sometimes conflicting plethora of options: "Dominate the Jebel area...counter enemy activity on the plain...prevent enemy rocket launcher attacks on RAF Salalah...cover the Sultan's Palace and Umm al Ghawarif Camp...carry out longer ops than 3-5 days... re-supply by air (with one Beaver?)... search grid squares... as in Malaya and Borneo (but there they had several brigades covering a similar area) training between operations...every base should have its own jungle and gallery ranges...move in a minimum of half-company strength." (Yes, but this means we cannot cover such a wide area.) "Wire in all camps...wire in the villages of Mirbat, Taqa and Aqwad...deny the enemy food and rice". (Yes, but this requires huge numbers of troops to cover the wire. Wire not covered by observation and fire is no barrier to the enemy.) "Prevent enemy re-supply...psyops...bribes, rewards...propaganda ops...destruction of the enemy on the Central Jebel, the Priority Task." (Surely not? Let's stop them reinforcing from the West.) "Western Approaches...enemy should not be allowed to build up their strength in this inaccessible area." (Hear, hear, I thought, may I have a division of infantry, please — two brigades for the inaccessible area, and one to secure the Lines of Communication to keep them there.) "Cut off the enemy from their base in Hawf and destroy them."

All this was good sound stuff but a most cursory assessment of troops to tasks made it clear that one could not, with four rifle companies, satisfy all the requirements listed in the Directive. It is easy to be wise after the event; sufficient to say that the task of destroying the enemy in the Western Approaches, allotted to my battalion in 1969, ultimately took some eight SAF battalions, supported by an Iranian Brigade and a vastly increased air, artillery and engineer effort, a further six years to achieve.

I could not possibly do all the tasks CSAF had suggested. Corran Purdon was more than happy to talk it through and we selected a strict order of priorities. I thought these should be:

(1) Keep open the Midway Road
(2) Maintain blocks on enemy West-East routes in from PDRSY
(3) Protect Salalah base area

The Midway Road was the main supply and reinforcement route from our own base six hundred miles away in Bait al Falaj. There was no possibility of re-supply by air or sea. If the enemy blocked the Midway Road for any length of time the army in Dhofar could not survive. This was the one task without which the others could not be achieved. It was in many ways the dullest and least adventurous task — and the easiest — but I made it the first priority because without its achievement none of the other tasks were possible.

To prevent enemy re-supply and reinforcement from their base in the Marxist-dominated PDRSY was self-evident, otherwise any action taken elsewhere in Dhofar was like mopping up a flood in the bathroom without turning off the taps. If we didn't disrupt or at least regulate the flow of men, arms and equipment, the enemy would simply grow stronger and bolder while SAF remained at the same strength.

Protection of the Salalah base was vital but I made it the third priority because it was the least likely of enemy options. It was protected by a wide, open plain and guerrillas do not like concentrating without good, covered lines of withdrawal. It was the one area where trained conventional troops with superior air and supporting weapons would have them at a disadvantage. I would welcome an adoo attack on Salalah but thought it most unlikely. What they might do, as CSAF had suggested, was fire off the odd rocket launcher or mortar bomb from a distance. Thus my initial deployment was as follows:

> One company — Ambush Corner — to secure the Midway Road and operate in the wadis to the east and west of it
>
> One company — Raven's Roost, the northern end of the Midway Road to operate on the northern edge of the Jebel and assist in securing the Midway Road
>
> One company — Defa — to frustrate enemy movement in the Western Approaches
>
> One company — Salalah Plain, secure SAF and RAF camps and act as Reserve
>
> Recce Platoon — to operate in the open desert over a wide area north of the Jebel

"Go west!" Mike Harvey had said and I told Derek Whittle, commanding B Company at Defa, to carry out a patrol in strength to get to know his new area and confirm enemy activity and strength. Within two days of taking over the position, on 5 April, Derek took out a half-company fighting patrol to a prominent V-shaped escarpment due south of his camp overlooking the vast canyon of the Wadi Sayq.

The country was thicker than anything we had seen before: rough, stony ground with shallow patches of red, sandy soil and huge granite boulders, as if scattered by a mad giant. All over, the thick thorn trees, never more than fifteen feet high but whose branches reached down within two feet of the ground. As you bent double to avoid the thorns plucking the *shemag* from your head or tearing your face, you had simultaneously to lift your feet clear of the rocks, treacherously close-packed to trap your feet and ankles. The going was slow and rough.

Resting after some six hours of this tedious progress, one of Derek's outposts observed an enemy section moving in arrowhead formation, wearing khaki drill and carrying Kalashnikov rifles. Derek's platoon opened fire with a Bren and two of the new FN automatic rifles. The range was three hundred yards and two enemy were seen to fall. Back at battalion headquarters I received the operational immediate signal; "Contact. 6 Uniformed enemy. 1 killed, 1 wounded. No own casualties. Follow up continues."

Jubilation. Not just the joy of first blood, but possibly, at long last we might gain some hard intelligence from the dead or wounded enemy. At the same time, warning bells rang in my head. Too often had a patrol returning to base after a contact been ambushed, its success degraded by losses close to home. I signalled Derek: "Well done. Take great care on way back. Take long way home."

I need not have warned Derek, who knew his job and had already started back for his base via a route different from his way out. The dead body of the adoo was loaded on to a donkey for identification by the Intelligence officer and progress was agonizingly slow. About one and a half hours later I received the half-expected op immediate signal: "Contact. Patrol fired on by enemy at close range on returning to base. Capt Brook and 3 men wounded. Follow up continues."

They had run into intense enemy fire from a group of adoo thirty yards away, firing through the dense bushes and thorn trees. They had seen nothing, just heard the deafening clatter of close-range automatic fire, which caused four casualties among the leading section. Derek decided that a further follow-up would simply risk more casualties; his men were tired and dispirited after such a swift reversal of fortune. They loaded their wounded on to makeshift stretchers made from blankets and rifles and started laboriously towards Defa. At 7.30pm it was too dark to make any headway so they halted to rest until the moon rose and they could make better progress. They started off again at 9.15pm, the rate of progress three hundred yards an hour because of the difficulty of carrying the wounded through the thorn trees and over the rough ground. At 5.30 the following morning Corporal Hamid, who had been shot through the eye in the first enemy burst, but clung to life for twelve jolting hours on his makeshift stretcher, died.

At first light a Beaver flew into the airstrip at Defa to pick up the dead and wounded. Once again the casualty evacuation time — the time between infliction of the wound and receiving attention by a doctor — had been inhumanly long, some fifteen hours.

There was a mass of lessons to be learnt from this minor engagement which, I was sure, was to be the first of many.

(1) The area below Defa was clearly thick with enemy, either as a main base or a transit area on the routes into Dhofar from the West. The enemy had been moving carelessly when first observed — obviously in confident possession of the area. The roughly built stone sangars seen by B Company indicated some sort of training area. Two sightings of uniformed groups 15-20 strong indicated some permanency of occupation.

(2) Derek himself and Patrick Brook had taken it in turns to move with the leading sections in order to maintain direction. Patrick had been hit in the first burst of bullets, luckily only a flesh wound in the arm, but it was dangerous for officers to be in the leading elements in such close country. There was a natural desire to lead from the front and to choose the best route, but, if one of the two British officers became a casualty, much of the cohesion of the force was lost. Better, then, to be behind the leading section.

(3) We must get light, collapsible stretchers. The normal issue were far too heavy and cumbersome in close country.

(4) Because of the thick cover and to assist control they had moved in file — that is, in two single parallel columns. This made an ideal target for an enemy ambush. Patrick thought the bullet in his arm had gone through a soldier in front of him.

(5) Casualty evacuation — as always, without helicopters, a nightmare.

Two days later the enemy attacked Defa Camp with 3in. mortars, LMGs and automatic rifles. This became a normal adoo reaction over the next few months, the fire being particularly heavy after contacts in which the enemy received casualties.

There was clearly a great deal to be learned about the enemy strengths, movement and intentions in this area and I determined to recce it myself with a view to a big operation as soon as practicable.

Meanwhile, it was necessary to cover other parts of the parish. No 3 Company of the Desert Regiment, under command of my MR Group, had had several minor skirmishes on the Midway Road. A contact in early April proved that the ordinary Jebali, armed with a No 4 rifle though not in uniform, was far from friendly and, when challenged, would react like a trained soldier. Two Jebalis crossing the Midway Road were surprised by one of the DR picquets, challenged and immediately took cover and opened fire. One man was wounded and taken prisoner but could give no real information about the enemy. He was a typical "fringe supporter" of the adoo — a term which was progressively including the whole Jebel population. A month later the same company was clearing the road, prior to a convoy passing through. This was a laborious process involving the establishment of small parties, never less than a section of armed men on all the high points dominating the road and, once these were secured, sending a mine-clearing party along its whole length. Even though the picquets were in position, parties of adoo (this time in uniform) would creep up from the deep wadis on either side of the road and snipe at our troops.

The next day, 6 May, Guy Sheridan, the Royal Marine, second-in-command of C Company, successfully ambushed a small party in the Wadi Naheez, west of the Midway Road, killing two enemy whose bodies yielded twenty-three batteries for National walkie-talkie radios, forty-seven rounds of ammunition and some useful papers. One of the dead men was a courier. A colourful pamphlet, printed in Cairo, proclaimed "Every man a rifle! Dhofar Liberation Front."

It was clear from these and other minor engagements that the enemy were both present and active in the central Jebel and we could not afford to take chances on the Midway Road.

It seemed sensible to mount some rather bigger operations over wider areas in the central Jebel to try to establish where the main enemy areas were. There was no hard Intelligence. The SIO (Special Intelligence Officer) Dhofar heard reports from various informers of enemy bases at map reference so-and-so but these turned out to be totally unreliable. Informers were given a fixed sum in cash for information but much of it was simply invented and inspired by what they thought we wanted to hear. However, the frequency with which the Ayn Arzat (a falaj of pure spring water particularly favoured by the Sultan) was blown up indicated the presence of a gang in the Jebel to the north.

Thus I set forth with two companies and my Tac HQ on 7 April and again between 22 and 24 April to try and gain information. Operation FIRST NIGHT was aimed at a reported enemy base some eighteen kilometres due east of C Company's camp at Raven's Roost at the northern end of the Midway Road. The plan was a simple sweep and search operation involving C Company approaching from the north of the suspected area, 3 Company of DR from the west and a half company of NFR from the south. C Company with my Tac HQ would establish a stop line to the north while the other two companies would search and sweep towards us. Any enemy, we hoped, would drift like driven partridges on to the stop positions.

The preliminaries to this simple deployment were long and complicated. Neither C Company's base at Raven's Roost nor 3 Company's at Ambush Corner could be left undefended so that the two Recce platoons had to move up from Salalah to defend the company rear parties; my own Tac HQ and the FOO and his party had to move up to Raven's Roost together with a Ferret scout car, which mounted a .50 calibre Browning, useful for long range sniping. To get this lot into position the road had to be "opened", picquets posted and mine-sweeping parties deployed along its whole length. Then, in order not to give away the impending operation to watching adoo, a bogus convoy of empty trucks passed down to Midway to indicate routine re-supply movement.

Finally we were all ready to move. We marched due east for some fifteen miles in the heat of the day. The ground was open and rolling, the grass brown and dying, strewn with rocks just projecting above the surface. This was the watershed of the central Jebel, with valleys flowing either side to north and south, small indentations here which would gradually deepen on their route south to become the cavernous Wadis Dut, Sahalnawt and Arzat, thick with vegetation and water holes. Here the route was narrowly flat; indeed a vehicle could pick its way between the rocks and gullies and we took a couple of Landrovers carrying water and spare ammunition, whilst we marched beside them. They would anyway be useful in the event of casualties.

After a blistering, boring march we reached our stop line about three in the afternoon and Nic Cameron, the Artillery officer, spoke some esoteric instructions to his guns tucked into a wadi some seven miles to the south. Soon, miraculously, the 5.5 inch shells were bursting in front of us, throwing great gouts of earth skywards in a blast of flash and smoke. I had rather hoped this would produce a chaotic flush of uniformed adoo from behind bushes and out of the rocky caves. Nothing.

We watched the panorama of rolling grass and rock stretching far to the south, the soldiers eating the dry chapattis they had stuffed in their packs at dawn and gulping great draughts of water from their *chaguls* (canvas water carrier). The heat of the sun had made it almost too hot to drink and it did nothing for the thirst. Some of them brewed tea over little solid fuel fires, scratching loose tea leaves and sugar from packs and pockets. After the artillery barrage stopped we searched the area. There were scattered herds of cattle meandering over the whole area, attended by unarmed Jebali boys and women and the occasional old man.

Questioned, they appeared bemused. Adoo? Oh, yes, they heard a rumour that some bad men had been around these parts some time ago, but they themselves had never seen them. As we could see they weren't here now. It was true. There was no sign of recent occupation. And yet Ewen Tailyour's company of the NFR had fought a pitched battle here last year and lost nine men.

We took two Jebalis along for questioning and they came without protest. At three in the afternoon we closed in and turned wearily for home. We marched until six that evening, posted sentries and fell asleep where we lay. At three in the morning I awoke, shivering, and waited for the dawn. We finally arrived back at Raven's Roost by three thirty the following afternoon, having marched some forty miles in forty-eight hours.

Both B Company NFR to the south and 3 Company DR in the east had had long-range contacts with the enemy on their way back to base. In each case small groups of five to twelve adoo opened fire from long range but seemed unwilling to risk a long engagement. There were no casualties. It seemed to prove once again that the enemy were reluctant to engage large groups of SAF moving sensibly in open ground. In thick cover, with good escape routes, whatever the odds, it was to be a different matter.

Ten days later a similarly abortive operation was mounted to the west of the Midway Road. Again, Tac HQ, C Company and 3 Company DR flogged out to the west of Raven's Roost and combed the area in the Wadi Rishm. We marched by night. When we halted every two hours, to rest and listen, it took only one man to fall asleep where he lay for the whole column to become separated, as the front half of the column moved on and the back half waited for the man in front to move. We marched, we blocked, we shelled, we searched and swept, we covered a huge area of rolling grassland.

It seemed that we achieved complete surprise by our night approach march, for the party of adoo which ran on to Guy Sheridan's half company at 10.00 hours the following morning were moving directly towards his positions, quite oblivious of SAF presence in the area. The Omani corporal with four men was amazed to see a group of adoo wearing khaki uniforms and carrying automatic rifles, water bottles and equipment, approaching his picquet, led by an *"ahmari"*[21] — a white man. The unfortunate corporal thought it must be part of another SAF company. He was not used to seeing a European face among the adoo. He shouted, "Halt — who are you?" and the European answered calmly, "Who are you?" at the precise moment the other adoo opened fire before running back into the wadi. It was a great pity that the surprise element prevented the capture of any of this party and we were left to speculate what a European could have been doing with them. It was assumed he was a press man of some sort. Sure enough, a few weeks later there was a most interesting colour feature of operations with the guerrillas by a German photo-journalist in *Das Bild*. This gave us more details of how the adoo operated than any of our formal Intelligence.

In early May the *khareef* came down and once again the crescent-shaped Jebel was cloaked in thick mist and drizzle day and night. The parched earth hungrily sucked up the moisture and the brown grass gave place to fresh green shoots. Visibility was reduced to a few yards. The camp at Defa was itself just outside the *khareef* line but this enabled parties of adoo to advance close to the camp without being seen and this they did, opening fire with mortars and automatic weapons almost daily. Hugh Affleck-Graves, newly posted to us from DR, took over B Company and Patrick Brook remained as second-in-command. Hugh and Patrick were constantly thinking of ways to outwit the enemy. There were a number of favourite fire positions in the 180 degree arc south of the company base. Again and again B Company crept out under cover of darkness to try and ambush the parties of adoo who opened fire from these positions. But it only took one enemy scout in the thick cover to report back by walkie-talkie any movement out of the camp and the enemy melted away, often to return when the SAF ambush party had got tired of waiting and started for home. The adoo became adept at this waiting game, often moving into the ambush positions just vacated and opening fire just as Company B returned to their sangars, the attack perfectly timed while the soldiers were exposed, unloading weapons and starting to cook a meal and to relax. On one occasion the donkeys, still laden with MMGs and ammunition, took fright at the bursting mortar shells and galloped off in panic. The medical orderly took a bullet through his haversack.

I became slightly obsessed by the continual enemy attacks on the Defa position and arranged to go on two of B Company's operations to try and find out more about the elusive adoo who seemed to be everywhere but impossible to pin down.

I flew up to Defa by Beaver with the faithful Dad Karim and the following morning we set out with B Company to recce the Wadi Sayq. Marching due west from Defa we hit an old airstrip, codename FURIOUS, in fact nothing more than a strip of flat, high ground from which the larger rocks and scrubby trees had been removed. No aircraft had landed on it for some years. About a mile to the south of it the ground fell away into the cavernous Wadi Sayq, narrower here than to the west below Defa but still a hugely impressive landscape like some lesser Grand Canyon, whose slopes and precipices fell away in layers like giant steps, massive slabs of stone, interspersed with thick green trees as far as the eye could see.

Hugh and I gazed at it in wonder while the company melted away into positions of all round defence.

"We should get to the bottom by nightfall," said Hugh. It was now four o'clock in the afternoon. Indeed it looked a deceptively easy descent but I thought he was under-estimating the going. The sun was already low in the sky, showing the wadi cliffs in dim relief.

We gathered the company together and started going down in single file, one platoon moving while the others covered it; this was bandit country and ideal for ambush.

Gradually the path became indistinguishable from the rock-strewn face of the cliff. It was quite impossible to move silently; the slightest movement produced a small landslide of stones and reddish sand. Soon the sliding rubble gave way to huge boulders, six to fifteen feet high and each one had to be negotiated with help, one man handing his weapons to another while he climbed and let himself down with both hands. Frequently, the way would become impassable and we would wearily retrace our footsteps, the whole unwieldy column doubling back on its tracks. The donkey handlers groaned at each new diversion and finally gave up. We would have to send them back with their precious loads and carry on without the Vickers machine guns and water cans.

By six-thirty it was dark and we were about one-third of the way down the north side of the wadi. We could go no further without risking broken limbs, and the thought of carrying a man was decisive. We put out sentries and slumped down to sleep where we stood, in crevices and folds of rock, while the sweat dried on us and the men grumbled away because they couldn't brew their tea.

We awoke with the slow lightening of dawn and stamped ourselves warm. At last the men could be allowed to brew up and we gradually came alive. The tortured descent continued, the pull on knee muscles of some twelve hours' descent made each five-minute halt in the hour a blessed relief. As the sun came up we saw the black glint of water in the wadi bed — so near, but we didn't reach it for another four hours. We stumbled down the last broken scree, put out sentries and fell on the water like savages. Herds of Jebali cattle stood in the pools up to their bellies, their mouths dripping with green slime. We scooped away the green slime and the water beneath was clear and cool. Nectar. We filled our water bottles and the soldiers started splashing each other, washing their hands and faces and rinsing out their *shemags*. Black-garbed Jebali women watched the cattle with a few wide-eyed children. We asked the usual questions: "Where are the menfolk?" "Away in Salalah, selling wood." "Some — that way" (a wide sweep of the arm towards distant hills) "with the goats."

A single rifle shot rang out. This was the normal Jebali warning that the *gaysh* was in the vicinity. We were being watched. If we went further or lingered too long we would run into trouble. Some two hundred yards down the wadi we started the long ascent. There was a rough goat track which enabled us to move in single file and by a different route from our way down. The sun burnt our backs and we halted every half hour to catch our breath. The path was vertical in places and progress interminably slow. There were stragglers. Hugh Affleck-Graves, a Royal Marine Commando who drove himself as hard as his men, shouted abuse at Staff Sergeant Nasir. "Close them up! Close up the Column!" "*Ta'aban, sahib.* They are tired." It was the first time in eighteen months operations I had ever heard an Omani soldier admit to being tired. It was true. Beards and faces were running with sweat, clothes stained black with sweat. I myself had never been so tired. True, I was the oldest man on the march and only had one kidney but was almost gratified to see the soldiers just as near to exhaustion. Soon we were halting every ten paces to rest. This made us vulnerable. We would be useless if attacked, so I ordered a halt and we disposed ourselves in clefts in the rocks, put out sentries and slept.

The following morning, refreshed, we had an easy march back to Defa, arriving in the late afternoon. So much for that sector of the Wadi Sayq: not friendly, but no enemy stronghold, no living or training areas.

The next sally was different. Starting again from Defa, with the minimum escort of half a company we marched due south and then into a deep, narrow wadi running east to west. Down its dangerous length for a bit and then again due south. I was aiming for the prominent V-shaped escarpment which overlooked the Wadi Sayq where B Company had had their first contact and where they had noticed stone-built sangars built by the adoo.

We marched all night and lay up for a couple of hours before dawn. Hugh had led us unerringly to the edge of the V-shaped escarpment and soon after dawn we looked down into the endless cliffs and plateau which formed the northern slopes of the Wadi Sayq. The view in the pearly dawn was breathtaking — layer upon layer of tree-covered rock descended into the invisible wadi bed.

About fifty feet below us the escarpment levelled out into a long, broadish plateau, about one hundred yards wide and perhaps three hundred yards long. Here the trees thinned and the reddish yellow sand showed through. We climbed cautiously down, for to be caught on this open ground would be fatal.

The sun shone brilliantly as we reached the plateau. Hugh had left a section on the higher ground to cover us and now sent small patrols to each point of the perimeter, where the level ground met dense bushes and low trees and the plateau fell away sharply into the wadi. My first thought was that the plateau would make an airstrip from which we could supply a largish force to make a base in the area, in Wingate's phrase "inserted into the guts of the enemy", but almost immediately I realized that it was dominated by higher ground on three sides. Even that one side which opened on to the precipitous slopes of the wadi was dominated by a spur from which even small arms fire could cover the plateau.

Another smaller wadi (which we had crossed the evening before on our approach march) ran along the northern end of the plateau and into the main Wadi Sayq. Behind this the escarpment rose sheer to its summit and formed a solid wall to any approach by aircraft. Across this wadi and some three hundred yards along the escarpment was a series of huge, open-mouthed caves in the main cliff. Mike Harvey had mentioned these but had not entered them. They were awkwardly placed, easily defensible and it would take at least a company, well-sited, to cover any approach to them with safety. But they were just the sort of place the adoo used for shelter and for hiding equipment and weapons.

Soon we noticed some low stone sangars built at intervals around the edge of the plateau. I asked Hugh if he had built these for emergency cover or any of his company's patrols into this area.

"No, those are adoo sangars," he said contemptuously. "Ours would be much better built."

It was true. The sangars were regularly spaced out but the stones were roughly piled, with large gaps and too shallow to afford proper protection; quite unlike the neat symmetrical walls our own soldiers built.

"This must be an adoo training area," said Hugh. Or, I thought, a permanent defensive position, covering the entrance to the caves. In which case we were certainly being watched. It was no place to hang about with half a company patrol. We started to climb back in the afternoon sun. I tried to remember every feature of the area: the long sandy plateau overshadowed by the main escarpment, the scrubby bushes and dense thorn trees on every side, the glowering caves whose black mouths threatened the whole area, the twisting wadis which flanked the plateau.

We would march this way again, by night, with three hundred men. I must remember every yard of the way.

9

In the weeks following our patrol to the Wadi Sayq B Company had six three tonners blown up on mines. Two soldiers were killed when the force of the explosion propelled them upwards head first on to the roof of the cab of the vehicle, but passengers in the back survived with broken legs and lacerations, thanks to the floor of the vehicle being reinforced with sandbags.

The company at Defa depended for its survival on a water hole at Mudhai some sixty miles to the north. Every three or four days a convoy of three tonners had to run the gauntlet of enemy mines, planted haphazardly along the route and, though the vehicles followed a different track across the open desert every time, the law of averages took its toll. Patrick Brook, second-in-command of B Company, always first to go where there was danger, was twice blown up in his vehicle and survived each time. I had a premonition that if he continued with B Company his luck would eventually run out. He was anyway due for a rest, so I withdrew him to Salalah and made him Adjutant in place of David Bayley.

Meanwhile, the adoo continued to attack Defa regularly with mortars and small arms fire. We deployed a 25 pounder in the camp and a Provost fighter from Salalah strafed the known enemy positions but any casualties caused were carried away by the adoo so that only pools of blood indicated any success.

I began to plan Operation LANCE, a fairly ambitious sortie south of Defa, involving B and C Companies, a platoon of DR, a troop of the Oman Gendarmerie (OG), the MMG and Recce Platoons and artillery and air support.

Once again, the move of this number of troops north across the central Jebel to Midway, west and then south some seventy miles to Defa, without betraying any unusual redeployment which would compromise a pending attack to the enemy, involved a lot of preliminary preparation. (For any reader interested in the sort of detail involved, I attach a copy of the Operation Order as an Appendix at the back of this book.)

The preliminary move from Salalah to Defa, staging at Midway, involved moving C Company to Defa, a platoon of DR to guard C Company's empty camp at Raven's Roost, a troop of the OG to Defa to guard their base while they were on the operation and a detachment of the Artillery Troop to Defa to give us gunner support. All the trucks had to return from Midway and Raven's Roost to make it appear a routine move to any watching adoo. Two days before this convoy was due to lumber up the Midway Road, the Ramp was blown up.

The northern limit of the central Jebel was edged by a steep escarpment, down which the road descended by means of several sharp bends and a steep ramp constructed by the oil company out of stout baulks of timber, like railway sleepers with stone in-filling. The enemy had laid some twenty charges of 5lbs each along the length of the ramp, some of which had not exploded and only caused some slight damage. However, the road had huge craters in it and was quite impassable. It was easy enough to repair; manual labour and two days would suffice. What worried me was the security of the operation. Had the whole plan been compromised, perhaps by some soldiers talking carelessly in the suq? Had a Jebali passed the word to the adoo so that not only were they warned of our movement but lying in wait? But if I delayed the operation now, the monsoon would be upon us, making movement twice as difficult and the vital air support impossible. The moon was favourable, rising early, to help guide us in the early stage of our march, but setting around midnight when we would be close to the enemy living area.

I decided to go ahead as planned. Fatigue parties worked frantically to fill in the craters in the road and by 22 May, the planned date, the road was open. The preliminary moves took place over the next few days. Patrick Brook, determined not to sit at his desk in Salalah while all this was going on, appointed himself my Battle Adjutant for the operation and flew up with Tac HQ, myself, Khalfan my signaller and a rather apprehensive Dad Karim.

Once we were assembled at Defa, I gave out final orders to the officers, the soldiers had a huge meal of curried goat and I prayed that the adoo would not attack while we were thus concentrated. They fired their usual few mortar bombs and light machine guns into the camp from a distance but we were all under cover and sustained no damage. The Officers' Mess tent was dug in into a deep hole surrounded by sangar walls. Nothing but a direct hit from a mortar bomb would harm us and we sat in the companionable glow of the hurricane lamp while Hugh's orderlies served us chicken and rice washed down with warmish lager.

The companies formed up for inspection, faces blackened with camouflage cream, every man made to jump up and down to ensure that no weapon or equipment rattled. One man rattled like a tinker — biscuits in his mess tin. Donkey loads were checked to ensure that they were secure and silent.

We marched. Hugh led with B Company. I moved with C Company. The long narrow wadi south of Defa (Codenamed "Dee") ran diagonally south-east, almost to the objective, the plateau we had recce'd with B Company some days before, which seemed to be the focal point of enemy activity. But the Wadi Dee was a perfect place for ambush and we followed it only for a short distance until we found a route up its steep walls. Then a gradually descending slope, covered with dense thorn and jagged boulders. Even moving slowly and cautiously we seemed to make enough noise to alert an enemy for miles around. Sweat poured off us; we stopped every fifty yards to listen. I began to regret the chicken and rice which gave me acute indigestion. Patrick Brook was indefatigable, checking the column at every halt by waiting for each man to get up and go past him before painfully overtaking the whole column again to arrive in the lead. He must have marched twice the distance of anyone else over that fiendish country.

We approached the objective just before dawn. B Company sheered off to the right to take up position at one end of the plateau. Tac HQ and C Company disposed themselves on the northern edge. Thus, by dawn I intended to be in good cover dominating the plateau on two sides.

Dawn. We stretched, shivering with cold, and checked our position. As the first grey light filtered through the trees we saw the plateau some twenty feet below us. Perfect. Hugh and Patrick, fresh from numberless patrols over the area with B Company, had led us unerringly. We were well disposed in crevices between the rocks and scrub, invisible from a few yards away, well protected from bombs or bullets.

Was B Company in the right place? We had observed wireless silence during the night march. At that moment Hugh Affleck-Graves came on the wireless from the far end of the plateau to our right to report that he could see what looked like two strong sections of uniformed men moving in file immediately below our positions. Was it us — or could he assume it was adoo and open fire with his MMG's? Incredulous that the enemy should move so openly in perfect formation and mindful of the difficulties of recognizing bodies of khaki-clad soldiers in dense cover, I told him to hold his fire until I had checked. Simon quickly confirmed that all his platoon were lying out of sight. But oh, the tragedy! By the time I have given Hugh the all-clear, the target has melted out of sight. (I spend the next few minutes bemoaning this loss of initiative — not to kill this elusive enemy but to wound and capture two or three who would give us information.)

0700 hours and the air strike was called in to try and create movement with fragmentation bombs. He who moved was at a disadvantage in this close terrain and now that we were sitting pretty I wanted the enemy to move first. Two Provosts fell out of the sky like darts. 250lb fragmentation bombs crashed and re-echoed over the wadi. The first dive produced immediate retaliatory fire from adoo LKGs below the rim of the plateau and from a small wooded hill slightly below my position with C Company and to the east. There seemed to be a dozen different positions firing up at the Provosts. We could see the enemy moving among the tangled thorn and a great weight of fire was brought down on them by Nic Cameron, the Artillery FOO, from the Vickers MMGs of both companies and small arms. Within seconds the surprised rebels had switched their fire from the aircraft to our position but they were outflanked and dominated by our higher ground. Their fire was concentrated and noisy but high and ceased after about three minutes. Small parties were seen running and there were cries for help from the wounded. Like the terrorists in Malaya, like all good guerrillas, they never left their casualties if they could possibly extricate them.

We had stirred up a hornets' nest. It was time to consolidate the surprise gained and B Company were ordered to clear the plateau, supported by C Company and the guns, whose OP had a grandstand view with my Tac HQ on covered ground to a flank.

We watch the first platoon skirmishing forward, making excellent use of limited cover on the plateau, 20 feet below us. Suddenly there is a burst of firing immediately to their front. Roger Brown, second-in-command of B Company, talks calmly on the wireless and reports that the platoon commander has been hit in the stomach and they are pinned down. Supporting fire is quickly laid on and the advance continues with the remaining two platoons. Again the rebels withdraw, firing as they go from thick cover at the edge of the plateau. Meanwhile, we have fleeting glimpses of other groups of enemy at varying ranges to the east and west of our position. Nic Cameron brings down accurate fire from the gun 6000 yards away to the north and we redeploy C Company's Vickers to engage them.

B Company have cleared most of the plateau, but have met more opposition at the far end. They are now out of range for us to give them close support, so a platoon of C Company under Guy Sheridan is sent to seize Tangle Hill, from where the enemy first engaged us. A second air strike is called to help B Company deal with the enemy in thick cover to their front. Guy reports pools of blood but no other signs of enemy on the hill and the rest of C Company move to join with them. At the same time the rear platoon of B Company are ordered to close on the hill and here their wounded platoon commander dies. I look down at the pathetically small bundle under an army blanket. Poor Staff-Sergeant Nasir, I had given him a fearful rocket on the Wadi Sayq for not showing initiative. He had shown it now. I wanted to say: "Well done," and "I'm sorry." The soldiers look away.

It was clear that the rebels were in some strength, very sensitive to penetration of this area and that the whole of B Company would be needed to escort their casualty back to the base camp. (Oh, the waste of time and effort but, like the rebels, we cannot leave our dead and vital men must be diverted for the long carry.) This meant that we hadn't the strength to carry out phase 4 and 5 of the plan, which necessitated securing a dropping zone for resupply at the end of a long, vulnerable axis — and staying in the area for another two days.

I decided to carry on with phase 3 of the operation, using only C Company, intending to cross the Wadi Dee and carry out limited operations against the rebels to the east, particularly the caves area, before returning to base. The whole force moved northwards to the high ground overlooking the Dee and suddenly came upon a rare flat, open space on a slight spur, not marked on the map. This offered a good dropping zone, easily defensible and I decided to secure it for an air drop of water and rations the next day. Tac HQ and C Company went firm and B Company started the long march back to base.

The enemy was still active and several groups were seen at varying ranges from our positions. A section, moving cautiously on Tangle Hill, which we had just vacated, was shelled accurately and disappeared into the bushes. We were sitting right in the middle of the enemy home base and could expect a shooting match sooner or later. I welcomed this but not before we were ready. Sangars were built in record time and DFs registered on the surrounding ridges. The area was covered in thick bushes and lumps of volcanic rock which afforded good cover and as soon as arcs of fire and fixed lines had been tied up we settled down to the serious business of dinner. Soup, beans and corned beef never tasted so good, doubly welcome since their consumption lightened the load of our monstrous packs. Simon Sloane produced a bottle of whisky from somewhere and a generous co-operative effort lightened his load still further. I sat comfortably with Simon and his officers in a little amphitheatre of sharp rocks, about the size of a child's paddling pool.

We remained at 50 per cent stand-to and watched the soldiers eating their singularly unappetizing biscuits and tinned fish, washed down with thick, sweet tea. Like their British counterparts, a good brew-up was the high spot of the day. At 1730 hours came the half-expected cough of enemy mortar. Charge 1. About 700 yards to the south. We had twenty seconds to take cover, but luckily all five bombs landed some 200 yards north of our position. The fire seemed to come from one of our registered artillery DFs and three rounds of gunfire quickly silenced it. Guy Sheridan led an immediate patrol to try and catch the adoo packing up the mortar position but found only unused secondary charges and fuse caps.

Stand-to at dusk and dawn and a quiet night. The adoo didn't operate very early in the morning and I was anxious to get the Beaver light aircraft in with its re-supply as early as possible to avoid their attention. They had twice hit the new Jet Provosts with small arms fire and the Beavers, on a low pass for re-supply, would be a sitting target.

There were two likely ridges which dominated the dropping zone and Nic Cameron shelled them before two platoons were dispatched to secure them. Further blood trails were reported from yesterday's action. The long high ridge east of the Dee was too far away for us to picquet so the Provosts were ordered to keep an eye on it while the lone Beaver came in low for its drop. We were very short of water and this was dropped first. John Moore, the DAA and QMG at Force Headquarters, had conceived the bright idea of free-dropping water frozen solid in 10lb ghee tins. We were short of parachutes and, anyway, had neither the time nor energy to recover and carry them out.

The first tin plummeted down right on target, but, in spite of furious crushing with stones, the great blocks of ice took an agonizing time to melt before we could decant them into the canvas *chaguls* carried on the man. The Beaver made three separate sorties of rations and water, flying back to Battalion Headquarters to reload while we anxiously searched for a rebel build-up. Then the parachute drop, slightly higher and more vulnerable for the Beaver, to give time for the parachute to develop. The only one which failed to open contained three dozen oranges I had ordered from Bahrein. The original orange crush, but delicious.

Still no enemy reaction. Three hours passed while the airdrop was distributed and, between greedy gulps of blessed water, we began to congratulate ourselves that this dangerous phase had passed successfully and we might move off without being hit by the rebels. Then the first round of mortar fire landed in the middle of our position, twenty yards from where we were working. Nobody had heard the first bomb being fired but there was an ugly rush from the sangars, while four more bombs hit the position. The adoo had certainly learnt from yesterday's ranging shots and these, fired at close range, probably without secondary charges, were spot on. Two of the bombs fell within three yards of 7 Platoon's sangars (which I had sprinted for on the first strike, but, like musical chairs, had been beaten to it). I went over to see the damage. Two men had light flesh wounds; the rest were giggling happily and Staff Sergeant Mohammed Ali was grinning through his huge black beard. (A hard man, he starts fasting three days before Ramadan and makes his orderly do the same.) I must have looked concerned for he shouted, "*Ma Shay khawf, Sahib. Kull shee zayn, Shay Harb. Maa shay mushkila.*" (Don't worry sir. Everything's fine. This is war. No problem.)

It was clearly time to move on. I wanted to cross the Dee and get into thicker cover before it got dark, then move again so that we could surprise the enemy in the morning. The picquets were withdrawn and we started to pack up. MMGs, mortars, ammunition and water took an interminable time to be loaded on to the donkeys, but finally were ready to move. Richard Kinsella-Bevan was left with one platoon to cover the move out and the rest of us moved northwards to find a good lie-up position before darkness enabled us to cross the Dee.

No sign of any enemy movement but they are watching. Once again we are accurately mortared, this time from two different positions. They have moved at least one group to the far side of the Dee but lower down than where we intended to cross. Once again the artillery DF silences the mortar fire after half a dozen bombs.

1600 hours. The long single file of Tac HQ and two platoons is just clear of open ground when the enemy open up from four different positions with mortars and heavy automatic fire. The noise is terrific and as I fling myself behind a rock I catch sight of Dad Karim flat on the ground, willing himself invisible. I shout for Nic Cameron, meaning him to shout back, but bravely, he rushes through the bullets to drop down by my side. The enemy appear to be all around us but I choose the north as the likeliest concentration and as always, Nic brings down accurate fire within seconds. Luckily, the adoo have left it perhaps ten minutes too late and though bullets whistled through our thin cover and crack overhead, they are mostly high and the rear platoon, with Richard Kinsella-Bevan, takes the main weight of fire. One man is shot through the groin and two more receive flesh wounds. The mortar fire was mercifully plus of its target. They estimated our movement to be faster than it was.

Guy Sheridan runs off with a platoon to try and outflank one of the enemy positions. Simon Sloane works his way back to the rear platoon and extricates it from its exposed position. Meanwhile it is still light and I sit down for a re-think. First, we are too spread out to mount an attack and by the time we get organized it will be dark and the enemy will have moved. Second, Nic reports that the guns are down to six high explosive and two of smoke (we have fired over eighty rounds in the last thirty-six hours) so we have no further support from them. Once again the need to carry out the wounded dictates a change of plan. I cannot split my force again and further operations north of the Dee must be abandoned. It is getting dark and there is at least one enemy position on the high ground ahead of us. While Simon closes up the column I get through to Ranulph, just outside the base camp, and tell him to organize 81mm mortar fire to give the ridge a good pasting before we move off.

This is the dangerous time. The enemy know we are bound to move roughly north-west and will expect us to keep to the high ground and some sort of track. Instead we contour up the west side of the Dee which becomes increasingly precipitous. The stretcher bearers curse and swear as they winch themselves along, hanging onto bushes with one hand to prevent a fall of 200 feet into the wadi.

It becomes too steep for the donkeys, one of whom, in spite of having had his vocal chords cut, for silence, started a weird sort of honking. One falls head over heels into the wadi and a box of ammunition breaks free and plummets down in the darkness, making a noise like a rattle at a football match. One of the donkey men says reproachfully that this route "is not good for donkeys" and Simon nearly strikes him. The whole column forms a chain to carry men, stores, donkeys and weapons up the precipice. We swear and freeze between exertion and rest.

Where the hell are we? My compass tells me our direction is roughly right, but we haven't seen a proper landmark for hours. The ground is continually rising, but there is a deep wadi across our front which is not marked on the map. I hiss to Simon, moving with the leading section, to bear left. He insists we are on course. Ranulph Fiennes has moved his Recce Platoon out from Defa to support us across the Dee at its trickiest point and I call him on the wireless to put up a flare.

It must come from over *there*. It does — nearly. Simon is perfectly right; we are on course. We have only to cross the Dee to be in open country again, but the Dee in darkness would be hazardous for a stretcher party. Anyway, we are too exhausted to go on. The casualties seem to be bearing up well, so we put out sentries and sink down, where we stand, to wait for first light. I ask B Company on the wireless to come out at dawn to cover our crossing the Dee.

Dawn, and the last few hours' march. Rest, food and drink in camp while the Beavers come to take out the dead and wounded. Muala Dad, shot through the groin, is cheerful but there is a terrible hollowness in his laughter when his friends joke about his manhood.

What did we achieve? Two days later Aden Radio reported wildly exaggerated casualties to the Sultan's Armed Forces (including "RAF Hawker Hunters" shot down) but also admitted "many casualties among our freedom fighters". We gained useful information about enemy strengths and dispositions. This was clearly one of their forward bases, a staging post between the main base at Hawf over the border and central Dhofar. We proved that a free drop of water, frozen in tins, reduces the time over target of the aircraft (good) but lengthens the time taken to distribute the drop to each man and renders the whole force more vulnerable to a watchful enemy. My pet theory that if we were well dug in on a spot the enemy regarded as their own they would be bound to attack us on terms unfavourable to them was only half proved. They attacked us with fire at close range, which enabled us to shell them accurately, but they did not assault us physically which would have enabled us to destroy them. My personal postmortem: had I made any tactical mistakes which caused unnecessary casualties? Should I have directed B Company round the edge of the plateau, in thicker cover, to avoid casualties? Perhaps, but the adoo were everywhere and would still have shot them at closer range without being detected. Above all, the frustration of operating in this fiendish country without helicopters. I wrote in the Contact Report:

"Once again the system of casevac proved not only to be inhuman but grossly uneconomical in terms of effort. The need to carry out dead and wounded limits the commander's tactical options and mobility and choice of route, and gradually diminishes his strength. In this case an operation demanding the preliminary deployment of 350 men, their vehicles, weapons and equipment over a total of five

17. Officers of the Muscat Regiment on CSAF visit to Bid Bid.

18. Dinner's nearly ready; eating goat off the hoof.

19. HM Sultan Qaboos bin Said al Taimur.

20. Salalah Plain: strike-masters in attendance.

hundred miles and six days, was vitiated by the necessary curtailment of the op from 5 days to 3." This and other evidence finally enabled Corran Purdon to convince the Sultan that helicopters would increase the operational capability of his forces and the first Bell-Agusta Jet Rangers were finally ordered.

A few weeks later I went home on leave, having written a short account of the operation for the *Household Brigade Magazine*. I played polo. As I rode onto the field, Ronald Ferguson said, "Your Operation Lance. Seems to have been a right fuck-up."

10

The khareef rolled in on the Jebel, as always, within a few days of the beginning of July, shrouding the high ground in almost permanent mist or drizzle and limiting any ambitious operations above the tree line, due to problems of re-supply. It was necessary to withdraw the companies on the central Midway Road although the Defa and Raven's Roost positions, being just outside the tree line could remain and still operate in the Khareef.

Many of the Jebalis moved down to the foothills bordering the Salalah Plain from which they could more easily sell their cattle and firewood in the market. Sympathizers and adoo moved with them and our plain patrols had numerous contacts on the slimy reddish slopes approaching the foot of the escarpment, where rough, temporary shelters sprang up among the thorn and scrub.

While I was on leave, the company operating from Haluf, west of the Midway Road, had contacts in the Wadi Rishm and killed one uniformed and well-equipped adoo — a curious mixture of Eastern Bloc and West European weaponry — Kalashnikov with bayonet and seventy-three rounds and sixty-four rounds of British .303 ammunition (for the Bren gun carried by his companion), a green British Army oil bottle and a toothbrush.

Another contact in the Wadi Rishm was preceded by numerous cattle, herded by a man and a woman, who approached the DR company in a concealed position. At two hundred and fifty yards the woman caught sight of the soldiers and shouted *"gaysh"* as a warning, whereupon the innocent-looking herdsman produced an automatic rifle from beneath his cloak, dropped to one knee and opened fire before running back into the mist. We had for long suspected that the herds of cattle and goats on the Jebel were being used as cover for enemy observers. What was the answer? To confiscate all the stock, imprison the herdsmen and further alienate them by removing their livelihood and driving them further into dependency on the adoo? Or leave both adoo and their supporters this additional freedom of movement and infiltration?

Further proof of the inextricable mixing of adoo and innocent was evident in a contact a few days later on the edge of the plain. Some fifteen kilometres north-east of Salalah a spring of pure water flowed from deep within the rock cliff. This was the Ayn Arzat and its clear, crystal water straight from the bowels of the earth was the Sultan's pride and joy. He would drink no other water. From the fountainhead in the cliff-face the water was channelled into a *falaj* system — an open concrete duct which ran across the plain to the Sultan's gardens at Maa'murah and thence to the village of Arzat and the sea. By damaging this *falaj* near its source the adoo and their sympathizers could hit the Sultan in three ways. First, they could deny him and his gardens a source of fresh water; secondly, the broken *falaj* spilled gallons of fresh water into the desert plain, where it nourished thick grazing for their goats and cattle; third, it drew increasing numbers of soldiers to the area as protection to the coolies who were sent to repair the *falaj* and restore the flow.

In late June, for perhaps the fiftieth time, the *falaj* was blown up and duly repaired by the usual coolies with military escort. Guy Sheridan's C Company, with Ranulph Fiennes' Recce platoon, spent a miserable two nights in mosquito-ridden caves, hoping to ambush the adoo who invariably moved in to smash the *falaj* as soon as it had been repaired. Sure enough, two armed uniformed men moved into the area to reconnoitre and perhaps confirm that it was unoccupied, then withdrew before dusk. The next day two more men took up position above the *falaj*, watched for some fifteen minutes and then shouted towards the east. Almost immediately several herds of cattle and goats appeared as if by magic from the foothills and were driven down to the rich grass. With them were several figures dressed as Jebalis and one man closer, dressed as a woman. The ambush parties called for a Jet Provost which appeared within minutes and fired warning shots with its guns to turn the flocks away. The ambush parties, watching this parade of cattle with an unusual number of herdsmen, assumed that it was another adoo attempt to blow the *falaj*, using the cattle as cover. The Provost was called in to strike and fired its Sura rockets. Three black-clad figures fell and the troops closed in, only to find, to their horror, two women wounded and dying and one slightly wounded. In spite of medical aid the two women died after some twenty minutes. The men — armed and clearly adoo — escaped. A Bedu herdsman with the cattle came over and looked at one of the bodies on the stretcher.

"She is my wife," he said.

Simon Sloane, with the follow-up company, looked ashen and said, "They should have stopped when we fired warning shots. Everyone knows it is foolish to run if you are innocent."

The Bedu agreed. It was the will of God.

The enemy didn't blow the *falaj* again for many months; nor did they use women and cattle as cover. But what a hollow victory.

Ranulph found a rough note by the tree where the *falaj* had been broken.

"Socialist people for the emancipation of the Arabian Gulf: This is a note from the rebel liberators to our brothers who are under the colony of a lower state of being, facing terrible pressure and opposed by the reactionary government and the imperialist colony who are always aggressive against the people. We shall fight by violence led by the People's Republic which represents the hopes for success and socialist unity to improve justice and standards. We are able to fight a long war and defeat our enemies until we are finally victorious."

It was not the tortuous jargon of the Party apparatchik that would influence the Jebalis of Dhofar; it was the presence in their isolated villages of stone-faced uniformed men, who had forsaken and mocked the Moslem faith, who beat and tortured their old men and bribed their young, before giving them a prized rifle and luring them away for military training in South Yemen.

I decided to get up in a Beaver and fly over the whole length of the plain close to the foothills, and took David Bayley, now my Adjutant, with me. Suddenly the pilot wrenched the stick back and we rose in a steep climb. Unseen by me David had indicated to the pilot that he could see armed figures. But now we were far too high to pick out any figures on the ground, so I asked the pilot to go down. He didn't answer but neither did he reduce height. I repeated into the intercom, rather crossly,

"Go down. We can't see anything from up here."

"Any lower and we'd be within small arms range," said the pilot. "It's far too dangerous."

"Don't be so wet. We're not getting anywhere up here. Go down."

Tight-lipped and very formally the pilot said,

"Colonel, I will obey your order now, but I must warn you that I shall take the matter up with my OC."

He then rather spitefully flung the aircraft into a tight turn and dive, losing height rapidly and then tipped it to port and starboard, up and down, in a wild series of gyrations which didn't worry me but made poor David, in the back seat, violently sick. He later told me rather aggrievedly,

"Actually I saw several more armed figures after the first lot but if the pilot was going to go through all that performance every time, I wasn't telling."

We finally got a good close look at the thick scrub along the foothills of the Jebel where groups of adoo camped with the Jebalis during the monsoon.

I waited expectantly during the next few days for a complaint from the Officer Commanding the Air Force but there was really nothing he could do. Corran Purdon had very wisely insisted that all aircraft come "under command" of the land forces commander, rather than "in support" which would have meant they could plead aircraft safety, bad weather, technical complications, cold feet or teatime rather than complying with the mad orders of some death-wish "brown job".

However, the amazing instructions given by CSOAF to his pilots not to fly lower than 3000 feet over suspected enemy areas (which included the whole Jebel) made it quite impossible for the Air Force to give the close and intimate support the infantry needed. The advent of the new Strikemaster Jet Provosts made this restriction even more damaging. Our calls for close air support simply resulted in one or two Strikemasters screaming overhead at 3000 feet, totally unable to identify a target on the ground or to differentiate between the enemy and our own troops. There was of course pressure on both CSAF and CSOAF from Waterfield to conserve and safeguard these expensive new aircraft by not over-exposing them to the risks of ground fire, but meanwhile they were no good to us.

This curious reluctance to get to grips with the enemy had

manifested itself in both Malaya and Borneo, where the reluctance of RAF helicopters to go into jungle clearings caused bad feeling between the ground and air forces — in marked contrast to the Fleet Arm pilots who would take their helicopters in anywhere. Certainly to the RAF career planning departments the only theatre that mattered was 2 ATAF in NATO. Here alone was where an officer could advance his career. Those RAF officers who volunteered to fly ancient single-engined aircraft against a live enemy in some of the most unpredictable weather conditions in the world counted for nothing. I believe that of the many gallant officers who flew throughout the Dhofar war, none was promoted to high rank. In contrast, the Army promoted five or six to 3 or 4 star Generals.

I took to leaving SOAF out of all our ground operations, preferring instead to move artillery along the plain, or across the Jebel to the north, from which either the twenty-five pounders or the five-fives could cover most of our operational areas and whose pre-arranged targets, in response to a single code-word over the wireless, produced instant fire effect in the general area of any enemy opposition.

Soon a worried John Cooper came to me in my room and reported:

"Colonel, SOAF are very concerned that you haven't used them on the last four or five operations and that they're never scrambled now when you hit the adoo."

I thought this might happen as I knew most of the pilots were mad keen for action and resented the restraints imposed on their judgement and initiative.

"They're no bloody good, that's why. Until they come down lower to spot the targets we're better off with the gunners."

John duly relayed this to the local air force commander and it had the desired effect. On our next major brush with the adoo, without being called, two Strikemasters appeared overhead, at tree-top height and strafed the enemy positions most accurately, again and again. There was a great deal of enemy ground fire being directed back at them and I could see from the tracer that it was accurate. I called the pilot on the ground/air net:

"OK — thank you. You are being heavily shot at. Go home now."

For the first time I identified the pilot, Mike Kelly, who answered gaily:

"Roger. Just one more run to get rid of these rockets."

Again they came in, against very heavy ground fire (which they probably couldn't see or hear) and finally forced the adoo to withdraw.

Mike Kelly, temporarily in command of SOAF in Muscat while his boss was on leave, incensed by what he saw as a loss of confidence in the Air Force and disgusted by any implication that the pilots were "windy", had determined to correct this impression as soon as he was able. He had thus flown down to Salalah and arranged to fly the next sortie himself — whether the army called for support or not.

The result was thrilling. The soldiers were cheering and waving their congratulations at this unheard-of display. I never discovered what happened to the ludicrous SOAF order "not to hazard the aircraft in low-level attacks on the enemy" but thereafter the pilots did all that we needed with skill and daring, and Kelly, for this and other exploits, got the Sultan's Bravery Medal.

The khareef covering the Midway Road released two companies for deployment elsewhere and, acting on Tim Landon's rather scant Intelligence (as opposed to his intelligence, which was abundant), I deployed A Company to Adonib, a natural defensive position in foothills at the western edge of the Salalah plain. It sat astride the main camel route in from the west and our hunch was soon justified when A Company's patrols, supported by the Recce Platoon, intercepted two parties of adoo in quick succession. From one of these, the armed escort ran away in the dark, leaving as our prisoners an older man and a young boy and, most important, a heavily laden camel. His load contained rice, ammunition and a quantity of gold jewellery and ornaments. The camel was christened Wally and wandered amiably around our camp for months.

The likeable Anthony Willets had recently been replaced as Sultan's Intelligence Officer, Dhofar, much to his — and our — relief. He had previously been the Technical Adjutant of a smart cavalry regiment and was a wizard at repairing the many pumps and generators on which our various camps depended. Intelligence work was not his forte, however, and, perhaps misled by his various unreliable 'sources', his analyses were usually fairly depressing. He would come to my office with an air of impending doom and announce:

"You must move the companies from the Midway Road and concentrate them round Salalah. The adoo are massing and there's going to be a big push within the next few weeks."

I longed for a big push. Nothing would have suited us better than large numbers of visible adoo concentrating to attack our well-sited companies, dug in on ground of our own choosing, with wide fields of fire and close air and artillery support. But I knew that the adoo, typically guerrilla, would never operate like this.

He also relayed rumours that the adoo had acquired multi-barrelled rocket launchers which they had apparently manhandled from South Yemen and set up on the edge of the central Jebel from which they could reach Salalah. We spent many fruitless hours searching the thickly wooded escarpment in a nine-kilometre arc north of Salalah. Eventually Anthony retired to more rewarding fields of employment and was replaced by Captain Tim Landon as the Sultan's Intelligence Officer, Dhofar.

Tim had left us after commanding the Recce Platoon to do an Intelligence job in Sohar, where he had achieved a striking success, foiling a major PDRY infiltration from the Trucial States, thereby nipping in the bud a serious attempt to subvert Northern Oman.

He had now been posted, a perfectly round peg in a round hole, to Salalah. Here his knowledge of the language, including the incomprehensible patois of the Jebali, the country and the people, made him an outstanding Intelligence officer. He quickly developed new and valuable sources of information and his advice on which routes to cover with our limited troops to inhibit adoo movement and re-supply from South Yemen was invariably sound and dictated much of our deployment.

The khareef had nourished thick vegetation in the foothills of the escarpment and this provided easier access and good cover for adoo movement on the edge of the plain. Throughout July and August our patrols made contact with parties of adoo from five to thirty strong. Ironically, the Recce Platoon, visiting a Jebali village to dish out food and medical aid, was fired on by a large group of adoo well dug in on the thickly wooded Jebel overlooking the plain. The guide, Said bi Ghair, the first enemy to surrender from the old DLF was shot through the wrist. He didn't agree with feeding Jebalis anyway, all of whom he felt were forced, through terror, to co-operate with the enemy, however well we treated them.

Meanwhile, Tim's Intelligence sources had reported that parties of adoo were coming regularly into Taqa, the coastal town some twenty kilometres east of Salalah, free of army units and with only one small fort garrisoned by half a dozen forlorn and rather frightened askars[22]. To garrison the town with soldiers would achieve just the sort of dispersion of force the enemy tried to force upon us. The village was of no tactical significance and the one coastal track to it from Salalah was permanently mined by the enemy. I expected some sort of diversion to be staged at Taqa, at some time, in order to draw us out along the mined track and into an ambush. However, it was time to inspect the approaches to the town from the thick cover on the face of the escarpment.

Thus it was that I set out one night with Ranulph and the "Fiendeen"[23] to ambush the escarpment north of Taqa. If the adoo were visiting Taqa by night for food and supplies — and sex — we might hope to intercept them on their dawn return to the cover of the escarpment.

The moon rose late and we moved in the Recce Platoon's Landrovers to a narrow wadi which crossed the coastal track about five miles short of Taqa. Then began the cautious night march across the plain to an ambush position about seven miles to the north-east. The Recce Platoon, a close-knit force of Arabs and Baluchis, had been welded by Ranulph into a fiercely independent and professional but rather arrogant force, referred to by my Regimental Sergeant-Major as "Quabila Recce" (Recce Tribe). They moved silently, without any verbal orders, controlled by a series of mystifying clicking sounds issued by Ranulph and his section commanders. They had operated independently over the whole operational area for some months and had developed an impressive degree of self-sufficiency and esprit de corps. They moved fast too and I felt embarrassed while they waited for me to catch up and offered to carry my pack. Oh, those night marches. This was a comparatively short one, but, with no responsibility for keeping direction or control, I found them interminably boring. I let my mind dwell on matters miles away in time and space from the job in hand. Great moments of polo: my first play — small farce in the vast opera house at Leeds: watching the awesome explosion of atomic bombs in the South Australian desert; home via Hawaii: forgotten adventures and absent friends: fragments of poetry — anything to alleviate the tedium of the march.

And we are here as on a darkling plain
Swept with confused alarms of struggle and flight
Where ignorant armies clash by night.

That was good, by my great-grandfather, Matthew Arnold. Appropriate too, to this curious little unsung war.

After some five hours' march we breasted the foothills to the dark shadow of the escarpment and climbed through the damp jungle of what was virtually the cliff face. In a mercifully short time we reached a barely discernible goat track — a shelf about two feet wide — some hundred feet above the plain and settled down to wait. The moon rose and one could see the ambush position was well protected by dense trees and shrubs, watered by the constant drizzle of the khareef, which even now dripped about us. No tea, for the Jebalis had got an acute sense of smell and hearing. As the night drizzle got gradually colder and more penetrating and the sweat dried on us, we gloomily ate cold chapattis, sipped water from our bottles and waited for the dawn. This was when we ached for a good brew-up but dawn was the beginning of activity and, sure enough, we soon spied through binoculars (the soldiers could see with the naked eye) a myriad of white specks spread out on the sands north of Taqa.

We watched fascinated as they moved relentlessly towards our position, their herdsmen yodelling from time to time to keep them together. Nothing unusual about that, the rich grazing of the foothills was just below our position, but their intermittent yodelling to the herd might also have been a warning to the adoo. When they reached the grazing the goats started nibbling but discreetly, gradually, the Jebali herdsmen coaxed them up the slope out of our sight until suddenly they were among us, hundreds of goats scrambling up the cliff and along the track on which we were deployed. The Jebalis feigned surprise when they saw us, first one and then another of the platoon well spaced out, hidden in the thick foliage. Then they smiled amiably while we explained politely that we were waiting for the adoo and they must call their goats together and wait with us so that they could not tell the adoo where we were. It was certainly suspicious that, with the whole escarpment to choose from, they had aimed unerringly for our position. If they were indeed acting as a reconnaissance for the adoo we could not wait long. The watching adoo would have seen them disappear a few feet from our position and the yodelling had stopped. Our ambush would be pin-pointed.

Compromised to any watcher, Ranulph rightly decided to abandon the position as quickly as possible. We were on the move in minutes, scrambling down the cliff, the goatherds with us, to the plain below. At every step in the open I expected to hear a burst of fire from the limitless wooded face behind us. I anticipated our possible reaction at each stage. If we were fired on now, we could still run back into the cover behind us and start a flanking movement to get above and behind them. Now we were too far out and too exposed. There was a small ridge of sand which would give us some cover. We moved in fast groups, covering each other and when we were three or four hundred yards on to the plain I began to breathe more easily.

Suddenly a long burst of automatic fire rattled out from the trees and spurts of sand sprang up all around us, far too close for comfort. We flung ourselves down and the platoon were quick to return the fire, while, section by section, we withdrew to a slight ridge of sand which gave a measure of cover.

The enemy fire increased, a mixture of rifle and machine-gun fire and it came from somewhere near our recently vacated ambush position, though for the life of me I could see no sign of man or muzzle flash. Fifteen men against perhaps thirty, caught in the open, our every move dominated; no chance of manoeuvre to attack them, low cloud inhibiting air support; we could only ignominiously withdraw.

When first pinned down, I had taken off my large haversack, hoping to make myself a smaller target. Out of the corner of my eye I had seen Dad Karim, my orderly, watching me as he flattened his portly frame ever closer to the sand. I had never seen him look so flat. He watched me as I wriggled away closer to Ranulph and I assumed that, before joining me, like the faithful if substantial shadow he was, he would pick up my pack. Not a bit of it. Ten yards further back as we lay behind our ridge of sand, I noticed it now quite alone in our previous position.

Now the pack itself was a prized possession, a beautifully balanced climber's rucksack with good straps and a light aluminium frame. I had carried it many miles, stuffed with goodies to ameliorate the tedium of long marches, hot waterless days and cold dawns. Even now it was filled with good things, a paperback thriller approaching its denouement, a flask of cold loomi, a tin of sardines and two bananas.

"Damn," I said and raised myself on an elbow. The firing seemed to quicken. Ranulph, five yards to my left shouting orders to his platoon, saw the direction of my gaze.

"I'll get it Colonel," he shouted gallantly and before I could say, "No, not worth it," he was on his feet, crouching over the lip of the ridge. The effect was electrifying. In the split second of his appearance the adoo fire redoubled, the sand all around us erupting in little splashes, like hailstones on water. Ranulph wisely retraced his few steps, like a scalded cat and lay again behind cover, just as I said:

"Don't bother; we'll leave it."

Gradually we withdrew. I was surprised by the intensity and accuracy of the adoo fire and by the speed with which they had concentrated to attack us. Two of the Recce Platoon were hit, but not seriously, probably by stone splinters from near misses. But we had been lucky. If the adoo had opened up at closer range, when we were only just clear of the treeline, we must have received severe casualties. We marched to the vehicles. The soldiers were happy and talkative, anticipating breakfast, but I was depressed at having been again outwitted by a clever enemy.

Back in camp I remembered it was 30 July, my birthday; I sent a signal to Force Headquarters: "Contact. Recce Platoon north of Taqa. Sunray's birthday marked by 21 rifle salute. Two GSW."

The Sultan's only son, Qaboos bin Said, lived — some say was incarcerated — in the fort in Salalah and some of my officers had been at Sandhurst with him. It was suggested that we ask him to tea in the Mess but Tim Landon advised that it would be better to ask the Sultan if we could visit him. I waited for my next audience and explained this to the Sultan and after a short pause he said slowly, "Yes — I don't see why not." In due course we received an invitation for myself and "some of my officers" to call on Qaboos and take tea.

Tim Landon and Peter Southwood-Hayton had been at Sandhurst with him and David Bayley, the Adjutant, accompanied me down to a wing of the fort where a slave ushered us into his master's presence. Dressed in a brown burnoos and white turban, Qaboos was an impressive figure. Immensely dignified, he moved gracefully, spoke softly, his dark brown eyes gentle, thoughtful and expressive. He had a deep, melodious voice and was quietly courteous in his manner. His study was lined with books and most of one wall was taken up with a highly sophisticated hi-fi system and stacks of records, mostly classical and band music.

This was the Sultan's only child; his mother was a Dhofari, of the Bait Maa'shani tribe from the Wadi Darbat. Educated in England, his father had sent him to Sandhurst, after which he had been commissioned into the Cameronians (the Scottish Rifles) with whom he had served in the British Army of the Rhine. Qaboos's knowledge of the British character and customs had been acquired over a long period. He had grown up in a thoroughly Western environment and developed a deep and enduring understanding of European values.

Rumour had it that on his return to Dhofar he had been received by the people in Salalah with such enthusiasm that his father feared he might inspire a popular uprising of Dhofaris and had thus curtailed his movements and confined him to the Fort. There may have been restrictions on his movements but he was certainly free to move about Salalah, meeting his father's official guests at the airport. Looking around his very comfortable quarters we could discern no sign of forcible detention.

We were, however, made aware that he was unhappy with the situation in Dhofar and did not agree with some of the repressive measures imposed by his father in the administration of the Sultanate. As we nibbled at the thinly-cut sandwiches and sipped China tea from bone china cups we talked guardedly of the war. Each of us wanted to enlist Qaboos's aid in convincing his father of the need for change; to lift some of the harsher measures on his people and to win their hearts and minds in the struggle against Communism.

Without in any way appearing disloyal to his father, Qaboos seemed to convey sympathy for our point of view, that he felt keenly the misery and hopelessness of his people and the need for more humane, enlightened — and above all more effective — measures to win the war.

We left, heartened and encouraged by this thoughtful and intelligent young man but depressed that he could do nothing to alter the course of events. We were not to know that within a year Qaboos was to succeed his father as Sultan of Oman, save Dhofar from Communism and begin to preside over the long renaissance of his country.

11

I visited the small camp medical centre, where Mohammed Ashraf, seconded from the Pakistan Air Force, presided over the sick and wounded. Although trained as a surgeon, he had no facilities for surgery and could only try to keep a patient alive with drugs, drips and blood plasma until he could be put on a plane to the British Forces Hospital in Bahrein.

Sergeant Mohammed Ali was the senior medical NCO. It seemed a quiet time and he claimed to be bored with little to do. "Come to the Jebel then," I said, half-jokingly. "Big road opening. Come with my Tac HQ. It'll do the soldiers good to see you out there."

Mohammed Ashraf's contract forbade him from taking part in operations but Sergeant Mohammed Ali had done his share of duty on the Jebel in previous Dhofar tours. Thus he joined us at dawn as we set about clearing the Midway Road for the first road convoy from and to Muscat since the monsoon began. In our absence from this part of the Jebel we were pretty sure the adoo had occupied all our old positions and we would have a series of little battles to regain them and secure the road.

The plan briefly was for Richard John's A Company to secure the southernmost stretch of the road and the first dominating hill on the escarpment, codenamed 'Fort George'. David Bayley's C Company would then pass through as far as Ambush Corner (roughly half-way). Simultaneously, B Company would clear southwards from Raven's Roost to Ambush Corner and B Company NFR would clear the northernmost sector, from the Ramp to Raven's Roost. There was also a need to change over the 25 pounder detachment with B Company, north of the Jebel and thus both they and the companies moving up from the south had a gun and its crew moving with them.

The first indication of trouble came on the wireless from B Company at 07.30 hours. They discovered that the Ramp had been blown in six places. It was quite impassable for vehicles and would take a minimum of ten hours to repair. There was an alternative route up the cliff side, via Haluf, some ten miles to the west, but this would take time to clear and picquet.

An hour later A Company, moving ahead of me from the south, found the road blown in three places, each cleverly sited with cliffs rising and falling on each side so that there was no way round. Luckily none of the demolitions was covered by ambushes and frantic coolie work by the soldiers roughly repaired them and enabled C Company and my Tac HQ to pass through. A total of five demolitions had been made over the whole length of the road to its north boundary.

Meanwhile B Company, clearing from Haluf down to the road just below Raven's Roost, bumped an enemy section which opened fire on the leading platoon at about 400 yards' range. Initially only the leading platoon was engaged but suddenly the platoon carrying the Vickers machine gun, somewhere near the rear of the company, left this position behind cover and bore down upon the enemy position. Although hardly conventional tactically this was entirely on the initiative of the doctor, Mohammed Ali, but the Vickers' crew quickly responded to his initiative (they had little choice) and fired long bursts directly onto the enemy positions. With this support the leading platoon rose from its cover and quickly cleared the position, with only one man, Zal Mohammed, being wounded in the arm.

Meanwhile, moving with C Company, I was approaching Ambush Corner (Arbur Kaguish) from the south. At 1220 we heard a good deal of firing from the other side of the pass and it was clear that B Company approaching from the north had run into more trouble. The Company Commander had adopted the usual dropping off of picquets as each "tactical objective" of the road was secured. As his final platoon approached Ambush Corner they came under heavy, accurate and extensive fire from five different enemy positions. For some inexplicable reason the company's vehicles including the 3 tonner and 25 pounder, instead of being well to the rear, were behind the leading platoon. Almost immediately the 3-tonner carrying the MMG, ammunition, stores and rations, was set on fire and the MMG crew put out of action. A strong breeze fanned the flames and the commotion of petrol tanks exploding increased.

Completely exposed to heavy fire, there was little this company could do. Moving 25 yards ahead of the Landrover and separated from the Company Commander, they could not even get back to it and send a message on the radio. John Green, seconded from the Royal West Kents (in his first day on the Jebel) managed to extricate the set and scramble the SOAF jets.

From my position south of Ambush Corner I could see and hear fragments of this battle and was conscious of the rattle of small arms fire and of a deeper, slower boom-boom-boom which sounded like a much heavier cannonade weapon.

This was subsequently proved to be a Russian 12.7 mm Shpagris heavy machine gun firing armour-piercing bullets from a range of about 1200 yards. A spent round was subsequently found embedded in the engine block of the burnt-out 3 tonner and this alone would have immobilized the vehicle, apart from the fire.

The crew of the 25 pounder managed to get the gun into action and fired one round before the enemy wounded three of the detachment from a new position and pinned the rest down from the rear.

The driver of the 3 tonner, Mohu Gazzi, with the utmost gallantry, climbed on to the top of the vehicle in an attempt to put out the fire but was immediately shot in the head and toppled to the ground. He was dragged behind a wheel and given first aid but died soon afterwards.[24]

At this stage, with support weapons immobilized and the 12.7 Shpagris firing armour-piercing bullets from 1200 yards away, supported by four other enemy positions, aggressive action by the platoon was almost impossible. Sergeant Hamed Xana, with the mine-sweeping party in front, left cover to tend a wounded soldier. He then started to move his rear section but, due to the continuing and accurate fire, was forced back into cover.

Meanwhile, Roger Brown the Company 2iC, had gathered a rear platoon from its previous position and moved to the enemy flank to engage some of the enemy positions. After about twenty minutes the enemy fire dwindled, Roger Brown directed an air strike on to the enemy and was then able to leave cover.

The fire on the 3-tonner was put out, casualties collected and evacuated by a Beaver flown into the Raven's Roost airstrip (five wounded of whom two died later).

C Company, moving up to Dhofar Delta (the high ground south of Ambush Corner) had encountered two more groups of enemy, as did D Company while securing the airstrip on Raven's Roost. But, apart from this, the day's battle was over. By 1500 hours the road was open and secure and the empty transport, mostly undamaged, passed through and on down to Umm al Ghawarif.

I moved by Landrover past the damaged part of the road to A Company's position at the southern end of the road and watched the big convoy pass through at 6.30 the following morning. Again the whole length of the road had to be checked in case parties of adoo had slipped in under cover of darkness in the night.

For the next two days the convoys purred up and down the road, while the protecting picquets dealt with sporadic and ineffective interference from the adoo.

Finally the companies withdrew to their bases on the northern edge of the Jebel and two to the Salalah Plain. It had been a more eventful road opening than any hitherto and revealed a new enemy strength and vigour since the onset of the monsoon.

There had been a lot of mistakes. In a long Contact Report I made the following comments:

1. "En activity in the area, after only intermittent SAF presence on the rd during monsoon period, was expected. Large boulders had been strewn along the whole length of the rd in addition to efficient dmls in five places and it is gratifying that these were not linked with prepared ambush posns..

2. Coy Comd, through long deployment in Western approaches, was not familiar with the MIDWAY Rd area and failed to appreciate the ground properly.

3. It was a grave tac error to have tpt so close behind ldg elms and mine clearing party, particularly when dominating ground was not secure. Equally the MMG and sp weapons should have been dismounted and sited tactically to cover the mov fwd.

4. Top cover was flown at 10,000 ft (7,000 ft above ground level) on the first day. This defeats three of the aims of top cover:

(1) The need for pilots to 'read' as much of the battle as possible.

(2) Act as a deterrent to the en.

(3) Act as a morale boost to own tps.

5. It is regretted that this report has exhibited a certain amount of dirty linen but it is better to wash this in public than whitewash it — if others are to learn from our mistakes."

On the enemy side, when I saw the Sultan he told me that his personal Intelligence sources had reported that our stop position on the western approaches had seriously inhibited the enemy build-up in the Central Jebel. Without this the enemy resistance on this territory would most probably have been even more effective. I was delighted that the Sultan had, after long opposition to this apparently useless deployment, realized its effectiveness. He also said that six adoo had been killed and four or five seriously wounded.

"I hear you had quite a battle on the Jebel," said the Sultan.

"Yes, Sir. They've got a b....y machine gun called a Shpagris 12.7mm."

"Oh."

"It's bigger than anything we've got." I almost heard myself saying in schoolboy petulance, "It's not fair."

The Sultan looked thoughtful for a moment.

"I think I have something you might find useful," he said. "What about a 50 calibre Browning machine gun?"

I said I thought that would do very nicely.

"I'll have it sent round," he said, rather like a Harrods salesman.

The time seemed right to discuss other aspects of the war. I told him I thought the road opening had revealed a better organized and more determined enemy than we had seen in the Jebel for some time.

"I see," said the Sultan. "The adoo have made a lot of progress in terrorizing the Jebalis — torturing them, stealing their livelihood, taking away their young men. They're very bad people."

"Yes, Sir, but don't you think they will gradually take over the whole Jebel their way? The people are too terrified to resist."

I tried to explain as politely as possible that he, the Sultan, must do something to help the people so that he was offering them a better deal than the enemy.

What they really wanted was protection from the terrorists, but since we could not do that, we could at least offer them rewards for information, give them financial aid on a small scale, allow them free access to Salalah to sell their goats and firewood.

"I see."

"And in the longer term commence plans for hospitals and schools and clinics. They are saying you spend the oil revenue on yourself."

This impertinent sally produced a reaction.

"I have got to stabilize the economy before I do anything," he said. "I must first buy gold. All my life I have prayed that one day we would find oil. If they had it in Saudi Arabia and in Iran I knew we must have it here. I dreamed of the day. I dreamed what I would do with it." Surprisingly he got up from his desk and crossed the room to a chest of drawers and pulled out a large sheaf of architect's drawings.

"Why do you think I did this? For the people." I looked at the heading 'Family Clinic for Salalah Town'. "And this, 'Muttrah deepwater harbour'. All these things I shall do when I have the money."

I had seen the beginning of the Clinic in Salalah, a stack of breeze blocks on which all work had ceased a year before. I did not ask why he had stopped work on this vital project. I thought I had gone far enough, so I changed the subject to something more immediate and launched into an argument for permission for our patrol to give the Jebalis medical aid.

"Just some pills for their fevers, dressings for cuts and above all Golden Eye ointment for early eye conditions."

Then began a long argument and finally when I said, "We would do so in return for information," he relented.

"Oh, all right. Try it your way."

I beat a hasty retreat. A heavy machine gun and medical aid were valuable prizes. In fact our patrols had been dispensing aspirin and Golden Eye ointment for months and I have no doubt the Sultan knew this.

In due course I was instructed to send a vehicle down to the Palace to collect the machine gun, which I handed over to Captain Spike Powell, a wizard of weaponry who had recently joined us from Oman. Spike was a colourful Australian with a relentless sense of humour. He used to say, "I've fought in three ....ing wars [Korea, Rhodesia, Vietnam] and I haven't been on the winning side yet."

Later he came to me and said, "The old bastard has given us a DP gun! It's ....ing useless."

I sent a message back to the Sultan saying there had been an unfortunate mistake, the gun was a Drill Purpose gun (the barrel was sealed with metal) and wouldn't fire a shot.

Back came the message. Please send a vehicle. Back came another .50 calibre Browning — a good one. Meanwhile Spike had drilled a hole through the barrel of the DP gun and test-fired it. So now we had two. We mounted them on two Landrovers and thereafter had a useful heavy support unit for our sallies on the Jebel.

Ever since Operation LANCE I had been determined to launch another operation against the adoo base south of Defa. B Company was still deployed in the west and I would again move C Company up to support them. The B Company Commander (an immensely tall officer christened 'Captain Taweel') was still in command of B Company, following a contact on Operation CONQUEROR a few days earlier and I was concerned about the morale and effectiveness of his company. Arab soldiers are brave and aggressive when things go well but quick to lose confidence in their leaders when things go wrong.

I explained to Taweel that I wanted to come to their position, close to Defa, and explain personally what I wanted to do in the next operation in the main adoo base area. I should perhaps have been suspicious when Taweel said, "Yes, please do, Colonel. I think they'd like that." He seemed subdued.

When the Beaver landed the whole Company was formed up in three ranks and I got the Sergeant-Major to fall them out and gather round me so that they could hear me clearly.

I explained in a carefully rehearsed speech how successful and 'startled' they had been on Operation LANCE; that we had killed many adoo and identified the main adoo base and staging post between the central Jebel and the South Yemen border; that I intended to go in again with them and C Company and try to do some more damage. Any questions?

During this presentation I noticed that instead of the usual alert and cheerful faces they seemed surly and subdued. Now there was an angry murmur from all ninety assembled men from which I was just able to hear, "*Ma maced narooh; ma narooh*" ("We don't want to go; we're not going").

I went on to explain that I needed them; they knew the ground

and had already proved themselves on Operation LANCE; I relied on
them.

"No, we're not going."

"We'll be doing the operation with C Company whom you know.
They too know the ground. I shall be coming with you," I added
encouragingly.

A great swell of murmuring and shouting broke out. I noticed the
eyes of the man nearest to me had turned red with anger.

"What's the problem, Sergeant-Major?"

The Sergeant-Major looked embarrassed and spoke briefly to the
men near to him.

"They don't want to tell you, Sahib."

"Well I've come all this way to talk to them and I'm not going
away until they tell me."

Another noisy exchange with the men.

"They would prefer to speak to you without the officers present,
Sahib."

This was quite irregular and I began to expect the worst. A
mutiny. I asked the officers to fall out. I asked the Company again
what the trouble was and a great babble of angry voices broke out
of which I could understand nothing.

"I can't understand if you all shout. Let one man speak for you
all."

Another uproar.

"They say they will speak as one. No man can speak for all."

There was a long silence whilst I thought what to do. Suddenly I
spied a solitary 160 pound tent (made for two officers) which was
used as a Company Headquarters.

"Gentlemen. I cannot understand you if you all speak at once. I
am now going into this tent. I will see as many of you as can fit
into that tent. I shall wait five minutes for you to choose who will
speak to me. After that — you know the penalty for mutiny."

I marched off to the tent leaving a torrent of argument behind
me. I waited in some trepidation. Finally, first one, then another
soldier edged reluctantly through the tent flaps. Then another, then
another, like clowns emerging from a baby Austin at the circus. At
length there must have been thirty people in that small tent.

"Now what is the problem?"

'Sahib — we will go into the operation, but not with Captain

Taweel."

"Why not?"

"He has a djin (an evil spirit). Since he came to command us we have had much trouble on operations. Many casualties. You were at Aqhar Jashim. You saw the trouble."

This was a poser. The conventional wisdom, the innate law, was that orders must be obeyed and complaints made afterwards. So far they had not refused an order but now, if Taweel gave one or I ordered them into battle under Taweel, they would refuse to a man. It had happened before in SAF in many well-documented cases. The law stipulated in such cases that I support the officer against the soldiers, but I knew that Taweel, by his tactical errors, had simply lost their confidence. I could not put the whole Company under close arrest pending Court Martial; I needed them for operations.

Which was more important, a stark adherence to SAF Regulations or the confirmation of pressure on the adoo? I made up my mind. Taweel would have to go. He had been on operations for over a year and could do with a period off the Jebel.

"Captain Taweel is due for relief of his command," I said, "Captain Brown will take over B Company."

"We will go with Captain Brown. He is a good officer. When will Captain Taweel go?"

"Today, now, on the aeroplane with me."

They all beamed and tried to shake my hand. I felt like a Judas. The trouble with Taweel was that he was not really a bad officer. Intelligent enough, enthusiastic, too enthusiastic, he loved his Arab soldiers, and would chat to them for hours, round their fires or in their barrack room, gossiping. While they observed the traditional laws of hospitality and welcomed an interest by their officers, it could be overdone.

I explained to him quickly that he was due for a rest and I was releasing him of his command. He looked shattered but resigned. "You will become my operational officer," a key job which would not involve him with the close command of troops.

Taweel's trouble was that, in spite of a paternal familiarity, he also treated Arab soldiers as if they were Royal Marine Commandos and shouted at them, which they didn't like. They were quick to spot a tactical mistake, particularly a violation of SOP (Standing

Operations Procedures) and if they liked the officer they would forgive him — once.

Perhaps I should have sacked Taweel, but I was short of officers and he could still contribute in an operational role. Moreover, he was a Royal Marine officer, a volunteer for the Dhofar war. It would be a pity to ruin his career because a few susceptible soldiers thought he was possessed of an evil spirit.

That night I drafted a long signal to CSAF explaining the facts and my reasons for taking the action I had. I hoped — recommended — that he would not require a full Court of Enquiry which would interrupt operations and waste time. By return I got a signal from that kind man supporting what I had done and approving the arrangements. Not for the first time I was grateful to serve under a commander who accorded priority to the main aim and was willing if necessary to disregard the book. In fact there was at this time of SAF no book, no manual of military law. Past mutinies had been dealt with by the officer on the spot according to convenience and common sense. Officers who transgressed were simply shipped home.

Roger Brown took over the Company and commanded it with *élan* for the next few months. Taweel flew disconsolately back to Salalah with me and I subsequently discovered the main ringleader of the trouble and quickly had him posted. We could now proceed with operations with all four rifle companies.

Intelligence reports now supported what we had experienced on the ground since the ending of the monsoon, that there had been a considerable build-up of enemy numbers and weapons. We had certainly found more mines, and more machine guns and heavy weapons had been infiltrated in from the West during the monsoon period.

It was now clearly time to think about going next to the caves area with two companies. Tim Landon's sources reported some new routes in from the West being used by the adoo, and it seemed that the higher priority was to try and block them by further reinforcement.

I therefore decided to deploy A Company in a series of concealed positions from the coastline across the plain to the floor of the escarpment, and David Bayley's C Company on top of the escarpment, in thickly foliated rocky terrain which folded down on the cliff face, another position with an early SOAF airstrip nearby. The open ridge to the West would be patrolled by the Recce planes.[25] This left one company to patrol the Midway Road in reserve at Umm al Ghawarif.

To enable C Company and the Recce Platoon to reach their positions meant the long diversion north of the Qara, and yet another opening of the Midway Road.

This was called 'Operation Conqueror II' and CSAF, always keen to be in the forefront of any battle, came down and joined up with the Regiment. A Company, under Richard John, set out moving by night so that they could secure Pt 461 before first light. This was a prominent peak of rocky ground which dominated the whole southern approach to the Midway Road which wound up from the plain.

Luckily A Company got there before the adoo and covered the rest of the Battalion moving up. CSAF and I moved up just behind C Company who were almost immediately fired on from the foothills west of the road. In no time CSAF was down behind C Company's Bren gunner, correcting his aim and setting his sights.

Luckily the Recce Platoon had moved to higher ground in an area 150 yards west of C Company and when the adoo opened fire they were immediately outflanked. David Bayley had wisely laid his 3-inch mortar on a likely enemy position only 100 yards short of the actual enemy position and the Sultan's precious 50mm Browning and artillery were also fortunately laid on the enemy position.

The enemy were then completely overpowered and soon withdrew. Meanwhile B Company, picqueting south from Haluf, were engaged by two strong sections. B Company NFR were engaged by two much stronger groups (including a Shpagri) north of Ambush Corner and had three men killed and two wounded. However, the road was safely opened and already independent reports confirmed six enemy killed and four more seriously wounded.

The redeployment of A Company, C Company and the Recce Platoon on the Leopard Line soon yielded results and confirmed that the routes were being used regularly by the adoo.

A well-placed A Company ambush engaged a party of some forty adoo moving towards them from the east in the early evening. They captured three prisoners of the adoo and an old man accused of giving information to SAF and, judging by the amount of blood in the area, wounded several adoo. The old man subsequently gave us useful information about adoo routes and resting places on the way in from the area. Meanwhile B Company under Roger Brown ambushed two men north of the Midway Road, killed one and captured the other. Again we gleaned some good intelligence, including the position of the Shpagri, guarded by about twenty men in a wadi north-east of the Agbar Yasmin and B Company NFR mounted an operation to capture it. They overshot the position and ran into some fifty or so adoo. There was a furious firefight and the NFR lost one man shot in the head.

These contacts all took place on the same day and indicated a general increase in the numbers of the enemy.

I flew up to David Bayley's C Company, now well-established in a newly built and concealed position with a deep wadi in front of them. After a congenial supper in a comfortable dugout we went round the Company's stand-to positions and I noticed they were well-sited and well-dug. There was a clear water hole in the wadi in front of their position and I thought they were set for a long stay.

That night I got a signal from Patrick Brook reporting that the adoo had attacked the fort at Taqa, virtually destroying a well and that they had killed some of the Sultan's askars who held it.

12

Peter Thwaites died on 23 May 1991, before he had the opportunity to finish this chronicle of his times in command of the Muscat Regiment. He had fought a debilitating kidney illness and all the complications for many years with his usual stoical courage and good humour. He is much missed by the many who have had the privilege and good fortune to serve with him.

The obituaries, the literally hundreds of letters which Jacqueline Thwaites received in tribute to an extraordinary gentleman and the influence he had on those round about him act not only as a monument to his indomitable courage and good faith but meant it imperative that the book was finished.

It could only be completed by someone who had served with him at that time and I felt deeply honoured and somewhat humbled when Jacqueline asked me to do so. It has indeed been a challenging and enthralling experience.

As the reader will appreciate, it is difficult to pick up where Peter left off — not so much because of one's memory of the chain of events that took place twenty-three years ago, but because he wrote in a most individual and entertaining way.

Peter Thwaites' period of command was considerably more difficult than might appear to be the case from what you have read to date. He was, after all, commanding a polyglot regiment, half of whom were Omanis from Northern Oman, who very often distrusted their mercenary Baluchi comrades. He had few officers, as emphasized in the photograph of his officer Corps. The local officers, probably one per company, had only recently been appointed, commissioned directly on the field of battle and untrained in the traditional sense. He had four staff officers and each of his three companies only had two or three loan service or Contract officers. He was in total command of a vast geographical area. He was directly responsible to the Commander and certainly, when in Dhofar, to the Sultan himself. It was the potential recipe for a right royal fiasco, added to which the military resources required were simply not available.

The enemy may have been somewhat polyglot themselves, but they were the spearhead of a combined Russian and Chinese communist thrust to take out the myriad Sheikdoms and Kingdoms in the west side of the Persian Gulf. Aden had been surrendered by the Wilson Government the year before and their tails were up. The aim — for them to seize control of the West's oil supplies; the aim for the Sultan's Armed Forces and the Muscat Regiment in particular — to deny them this ambition.

In high mountains above the Salalah Plain, the chosen home of the Sultan, and the indigenous Dhofari tribes' main agricultural, fishing and cultural centre, a battle, indeed a war, was fought against a determined guerrilla enemy by a band of mercenaries commanded by a quintessential Grenadier, aided by seven British loan service officers. There was support but it was extremely limited and seldom included the resources of the West, personified by a British Government that was paralysed in the definition of its responsibilities, if any, and certainly its ambitions and priorities.

We all remember a heart-breaking situation when Richard John, a British Loan Service Company Commander, was badly wounded in a skirmish three thousand feet up in the mountains and had to be brought out by stretcher bearers and donkeys — a strength-sapping journey of some twelve hours across deep wadis and some of the most inhospitable country in the world. All this in full view of four British warships including *Hermes,* the helicopter carrier, steaming off-shore on the borderline between Oman and the Aden Hadhramaut, who were forbidden to come to our aid and could so easily have sent in a helicopter to pull him out. The fact that he did not die was due to Peter's leadership, not the mind-boggling inactivity of the powers that be.

13

In the middle of August, 1969, Peter took some much needed leave and handed over command of the Muscat Regiment to his vastly experienced second-in-command, Major John Cooper, DCM, MBE. John was a contract officer who had spent all his life since joining the Scots Guards in 1940 on active service of one sort or another. David Stirling's driver in the early days of the SAS, he then went off on SOE[26] operations in France, was commissioned into the SAS, fought through the Malayan Emergency and had even taken part in the Jebel Akhdar war when the Sultan needed help from the British Government to put down the insurrection of the Imam. This involved two squadrons of SAS scaling, by night, the 10,000-foot-high fortress occupied by the rebels in the Northern Oman, an heroic effort. Since then, John had become a mercenary and had been involved in most of the world's troublespots, including South Yemen, where he had picked up his incomprehensible Arabic; at least it was to the Omani.

Peter virtually had to be dragged on to the Dakota which would take him up to Muscat for transfer on to Gulf Aviation and then home via Bahrain or Beirut. Beirut was a popular night stop for young officers going on leave. We were relatively well paid (£3,000 per annum) and a few, having saved their shekels for nine months, lost most of it on the gaming tables and in the pursuit of the abundant, if somewhat swarthy, fairer sex. David Bayley once worked out that he had spent in one night in Beirut at the then equivalent of the spending power of an individual earning £730,000 per annum; that is, he lost the lot!

It was extremely difficult for commanding officers to take any leave and certainly almost impossible to be able to plan it. Seconded officers were normally entitled to one month's leave for every nine months of their eighteen month tour; in other words, a month in the middle. COs normally did a three-year tour and, with the operational commitments, limited officer back-up and movement of their regiments from the relative tranquillity of the north to the hectic operations in the south, it became a planning nightmare.

The operational plans for the period of Peter's leave were well established. We had just completed a period – post monsoon – of fairly major operations and a period of consolidation was required for administration, more battle training and some rest and recuperation. In the three-week period Peter was away, the two companies on the Jebel at Raven's Roost and Defa, continued their day and night patrols, always trying to leave ambush parties in position to catch the unwary adoo.

The company based on the plain became the real operational unit which particularly suited John's experience and innovative skills. Landrovers started to bristle with weapons, sourced mainly from the Sultan's private supply. Vehicles were mine-proofed with sandbags and we became an ever more mobile force. The adoo were becoming increasingly proficient in mining the tracks that existed, so we took off into the open spaces wherever we could. We had, of course, to protect the strategic targets on the Plain and, having all the advantages of mobility, better communications and support weapons, what initiatives the adoo took were quickly countered. These were mostly long-range pot shots at serving RAF personnel, at RAF Salalah (which amused us), and foolhardy efforts to destroy the Sultan's private water supply at Ayn Arzat which watered his luscious gardens at Maa' murah. It was all pretty predictable and more and more devious plans were devised to catch out the adoo. All the routes from the Jebel converged on Salalah like a spider's web, and with well-planned ambushes, increasingly better intelligence and our imposing and hostile mobility we were confident of control and limited success.

Peter's leave must have been particularly successful for he returned looking somewhat paler but full of new ideas and enthusiasm for the job in hand. The end of his tour was in sight – some six months away – and he was determined that SAF and particularly his beloved Muscat Regiment would prosper. A sea change in tactics and even strategy was also the product of a break from the front line and a little time to think things out.

I left, after commanding C Company for two and a half years and David Bayley, the Adjutant, took over - somewhat to the chagrin of Guy Sheridan, who had, after all, been second-in-command for a year and was very experienced. Maybe his Arabic, which was dreadful, was not up to scratch. Guy later commanded the task force that took South Georgia in the Falkland War. Prior to leaving the Army, I then went on a recruiting tour of the UK, to Sandhurst, the Staff College and young officers courses, to drum up new recruits for a period of secondment with SAF. Peter was very keen to try and attract the widest recognition of what was going on in Oman and the more volunteers that could enter the selection procedure the better the MR, SAF and the Oman. He thought we had been clandestine quite long enough. A new regiment was about to be formed and obviously the whole war was going to escalate. The quality of the seconded British officers would be all-important to the success or failure of the campaign.

Immediately Peter returned he was off to visit the companies, flying up by Beaver to Raven's Roost and Defa and travelling by Landrover to see the various Salalah Plain positions. He was keen to find out what had been going on and anxious to test his theories with his younger officers actually in the front line. His efforts to find the Recce Platoon must have tested his patience somewhat. They were somewhere north of the Jebel but quite where even their Commander was not quite sure. For a Commanding Officer Peter was unusually skilled at questioning his officers. Very often they did not even realize their opinions were being sought. He would listen carefully and one knew that a well-thought-out and clearly presented argument would have a fair hearing. There were standards on which he was not prepared to compromise but he was very aware that his young officers bore the brunt of the harsh and somewhat dangerous conditions under which we operated and that their support and understanding were imperative to the success of MR.

Whenever a company strength operation took place, Peter would insist on coming along as an 'observer'. "Don't worry, old chap, I won't interfere or get in the way."

He would fly in the previous day by Beaver to the nearest airstrip, clutching the latest UK papers, mail and essential supplies, a cold bag of delicious goodies and the inevitable beer, whisky and Australian red wine. His orderly would be equally weighed down clutching numerous chaguls of fresh cool water - these were definitely not for our consumption. I think we were all too young and self-centred to appreciate that the arduous patrols and operations took their toll on his health and he was anyway some twenty years older than most of us. The water was absolutely essential for him and he drank gallons of it. On the occasions when we were short of it - frequently - he really did suffer and after a three-thousand-foot steep climb at night he would often be the worse for wear. He never complained and would recover quickly after a cup of tea and the inevitable cigarette.

The "I'm only an observer" routine fooled no one and somewhat heated words took place occasionally between Peter and his officers as to who was actually in control. The Royal Navy have always had a rather better system in this regard - the ship's captain is in control regardless of rank.

It is difficult to describe the country over which we operated. The Jebel Companies were on top of the mountain range but as far as could be seen it appeared to be a fairly flat plateau - odd bits of higher ground and it was only as we moved across that plateau that at least every mile one would come across a deep wadi, often two to two and a half thousand feet deep - densely covered with thorn and frankincense bushes and mostly running north to south. These wadis had to be crossed and it was a supreme test of fitness and perseverance. Few of us had any experience of this type of operation or terrain and we adopted similar tactics to those used by the Indian Army on the Khyber Pass; always one foot on the ground - picketing all the way - cover of one position by another and take your time. It was ideal country for guerrilla warfare. One man could engage us from a distance of five hundred yards - from the other side of a wadi and there was no way we could get to grips with him. Without helicopters, it was perhaps a two- or three-hour task to traverse from one side to the other. We all got pretty fit. The Omani soldiers were mostly hill men from the North where the mountains were much higher. The Baluch were all hill men and their ability to climb and descend at speed and with little exertion was a skill we never approached. It must have been hell for Peter - but we did not know it then.

21. A sangar on top of the Dhofar mountains.

22. A donkey wallah collecting the evening fuel. CSM Karim Bux looks on.

23. An observation post looking west: typical Jebel terrain.

24. After Sunday luncheon. *Left to right:* Patrick Brook, David Bayley, Lawrie Lawrence, John Cooper, Ranulph Fiennes.

The soldiers were well and regularly fed by the Army and they put on weight and muscle at an encouraging rate, rather like young racehorses. We were bombarded from time to time by propaganda on Aden radio which would go into some detail as to the fate awaiting any British officer caught in the Dhofar mountains. The Dhofari women had particularly unpleasant ways of dealing with the Nazarene and if they did not get their hands on you first the thought of public decapitation in Taqa was enough to concentrate the mind most beautifully. The loyalty of the soldiers was not normally in question but their ability to run up hill and particularly down hill at speed kept us on our toes. Quite what they might have done to a captured British Commanding Officer beggars belief!

When Peter arrived to take over command, I think he was shocked by the conditions under which his precious few officers were expected to thrive. It was alien to his Foot Guards background and certainly to his innate understanding of what was required. He immediately did two things: exerted his own standards on our appearance and insisted that the Officers' Mess, whether located in the relative comfort of Umm al Gwarif or perched on top of the Jebel, would bear favourable comparison with Chelsea Barracks.

We had all grown beards on the basis that water was short and more importantly that most of the soldiers had one and we did not wish to stand out as more of a target to the adoo than absolutely necessary. Picking up a white face in a telescopic sight was considered too easy by far. Peter exerted his authority - beards were out, with immediate effect. Representations were made as to our logic and countered calmly with reasoned argument. Our protestations failed on the grounds that firstly we could dry-shave and secondly we could cover our faces with the MR green Shemagh. It was a test of resolve which we lost in double quick time. Guy Sheridan remembers it well:

'The picketing was complete, the airstrip thus secure, the Beaver appeared. We had just completed an operation to the East with the CO, Peter Bennett and our enthusiastic gunner, Nic Cameron. Simon and I had gone past the designer stubble stage in an effort to emulate the year's growth on the head and face of Jeremy Lee and Adrian Wray, our NFR predecessors, and anyway we had achieved a headstart on the company barber for 6-8 weeks before we left Rostaq.

'The Beaver brought the mail and some bacon I recall. One letter was addressed to me. I neither recognised the writing nor the expensive envelope but I noticed it had not come far. Undaunted, I opened it and pulled out the headed notepaper of the Commanding Officer of the Muscat Regiment. The message was clear in its simplicity.

Guy,

'There is a faint, but appreciable, resemblance between yourself and an apostle. Please get a haircut.

Peter

"'What style!"' I pondered as I called for the company barber.'

Improving the Mess standard had our whole-hearted support. Peter insisted crayfish were acquired on a daily basis from the regimental fish supplier. They were normally thrown away by the locals but to us they were transformed by our Goanese cooks into the most delicious crayfish cocktail, or thermidor. Food improved. We were weaned off endless cans of cooled lager and started to drink whisky and soda and wine. Some of us took it a little too literally and had to be spirited off, back to the UK, such as one not-so-young officer who managed to lock himself in the deep freeze when searching for his early morning vodka and tonic. Most of us, however, really appreciated the improvement and much more the manifestation that Peter really cared about our welfare. He set high standards and expected the same in return.

It was relatively easy for the commanding officer to retreat to the privacy of his own quarters - a comfortable bungalow - but Peter insisted every evening that those officers not on patrol should have dinner together in the Mess and he would be there. A cool glass of something and a beautifully prepared and served meal was a tremendous tonic to the somewhat exhausted and nervously strained young officers. Nothing was too much trouble. After dinner there would always be a game of poker, not particularly skilful but nevertheless competitive. Peter with the perceived King's Ransom of Seconded Colonel's pay was considered fair game for his relatively impoverished young officers. A mess betting book was introduced and even the most frugal officers, such as Ranulph Fiennes and Guy Sheridan, would take on the professionals, desperately intent on saving yet more money. Initially we did well, having little to lose, but gradually experience and cunning, not to say nerves, prevailed. John Cooper recalls:

"Peter and I kept losing but over the weeks we got the measure of these youngsters and they became rather reluctant to play against the oldies."

We really did lead the most frenetic lifestyle. It was *de rigueur* to return from operations, frequently with little sleep over an extended period, and not to miss dinner. It simply was not on. In a totally wartime setting we would be offered duck shooting, swimming and parties with almost gay abandon. At the drop of a hat, however, we would be off back on operations to support those under fire. It was exhilarating and bound us all together like the Famous Five or the Three Musketeers, the latter probably being more appropriate.

The Guards regiments have always had a reputation for catering at a lush standard to the whims of its officers, even when on operations. Peter was keen to maintain this tradition. We already travelled with our orderlies, but in the more static positions we were now given one of the Goanese cooks and a Sweeper to keep everything neat and tidy. Tablecloths appeared and, while regimental silver was not provided, we tried to maintain a competitive edge over the facilities provided by the other units. We even went to some lengths to improve the sanitation. The soldiers would go off into the surrounding area to perform the calls of nature and used a stone instead of the Western solution of toilet paper. All very efficient.

Guy Sheridan had the camp carpenter knock up a rather splendid Elsan contraption and, on one of Peter's frequent visits, it was decided to play an imperial prank on the CO. He was due to arrive the next day on a three-day operation to stir up the enemy in the Wadi Jaheez area. Guy collected a handful of roundish stones from the surrounding area and penned out a notice to append to the seat of the Elsan.

"Please do not drop stones into the Elsan.

"Cast used stones to the left to avoid mixing with fresh ones from the right. The sweeper cannot manage the extra weight."

The loo paper was removed and replaced by a score of round stones. The CO arrived that evening and delivered his orders for the operation before dinner. "Stand To" the next morning was at the usual time and was followed by breakfast in a mess tent that resembled Knightsbridge Regimental Mess complete with a clutch of *Tatler, Country Life, Horse and Hound* and a few back copies of the airmail edition of *The Times*, very generously brought up by the CO from Umm al Ghawarif. These were pushed to the end of the table to make way for the company crockery and a sumptuous feast of bacon and eggs.

Guy Sheridan's recollection was:

"The operation began at 10 o'clock but not before the CO's body clock chimed a need for the Elsan. Rather cheekily, I suppose, Simon and I watched him amble up to the hessian and disappear. It was not long before the silence and our transfixation on the left hand side for an expected parabola of a cast stone was shattered by an order:

'Guy, fetch me two editions of *The Times*, would you, old chap'"

During this period of Peter's command he was increasingly involved in the political pressures that were brought about by being the military 'King' of the Dhofar who was still required to act in both the best interest of the Sultan and Her Majesty's Britannic Government. The former was in many ways the more important for, by fulfilling his responsibilities to the Sultan, he at the same time fulfilled his innate allegiance to Her Majesty The Queen.

Correspondence with the Palace took place on an almost daily basis and, while in the main it was concerned with the strategic requirements of the Sultanate, it often dealt with seemingly trivial problems of the welfare of a particular individual and his family. Peter never allowed this aspect of his command to be transmitted to his subordinate officers. He dealt with every request personally and it must have been a particularly trying aspect of his command. At the same time he had the responsibility to provide information on an hourly basis to the Commander of SAF, Brigadier Corran Purdon, who, quite understandably, wanted to be continually at the sharp end in Dhofar and be responsible for such liaison as was required with the Sultan. It was a predicament that would test the loyalty of an attaché and the diplomatic skill of an ambassador.

The Intelligence and political reports that landed on various desks in Whitehall simply determined that the problems in Dhofar were never as quiet as some may have wished. We therefore subsequently became very much one of the places which travelling political or military dignitaries always put on their proposed itinerary. To a certain extend we did not mind this, as it was in the generally perceived best interest of Oman that the more people who were informed of the situation, the more support, of all types, we would receive. It was not an integral part of the plan but it was used to our advantages wherever possible. High-powered political figures appeared on the 'just passing through' scenario but they were increasingly well-briefed prior to their arrival and their questioning of all and sundry became more and more focused. Deputy heads of Military Directorates found it slightly more difficult to get approval for their annual visits but their superiors appeared more frequently.

With the somewhat divided loyalties of the seconded Commanding Officers, and indeed the SAF Commander himself, it became something of a problem. They had to maintain all the operational priorities but, at the same time, to interact with some extremely intelligent passing observers who were of necessity looking more closely at the problem from their own vested national interest point of view rather than whether they liked, were loyal to, or indeed shared the aspirations of the Sultan. It was proved time and again that all these vested interests were best served by providing whatever support was necessary and possible to the Sultan's Armed Forces. More clandestine opinions and ideas were firmly sat upon by Corran Purdon and Peter Thwaites. There was a political, feudal and workable infrastructure that would, in their opinion, eventually prevail and it was not to be diverted by the political, military or personal ambitions of the roving ambassador. We were, after all, some twenty years ahead of the Kissinger approach.

Peter's intense loyalty to the Sultan may have been personal but it was more to do with an inbred principle that persuaded him that it was the only course.

On one occasion his junior gungho officers spent a week plotting the overturn of the Wilson Government, albeit late at night, somewhat inebriated and definitely exhausted by constant contact with the adoo. We had specifically worked out who would be involved, where to put the tanks in Whitehall and generally rounded off a near-perfect plan. With considerable enthusiasm we presented a coherent briefing to Peter, after a particularly friendly dinner, only to be given the most serious lecture on our responsibilities as Officers of the Queen and of the Sultan. What had initially appeared to us a bit of fun and then, over a period, a feasible operation struck him as a piece of stupidity at best, or treason at worst. We went to bed early with a particularly royal flea in our romantic ears.

Loyalty, we learnt, went both ways - up and down. Peter's loyalty to the Sultan, as a titular figure, was absolute. We knew from our own experience that his loyalty to us - his junior officers, somewhat prone to the occasional error - was equally absolute. On any census this would probably be the greatest denominator of all our opinions and thoughts. With the value of hindsight it was perhaps an impossible role to play but play it he did, and so well.

The role would probably have been easier if he could occasionally have bent the ear of a passing trusted journalist. They were, however, absolutely barred from Oman, which may have been either the most perspicacious decision of the Sultan or the one that cost him his throne. If trusted, journalists can of course be an advantage when you wish to put a point of view that may be a little bit contentious or provocative. This chance was simply not available and, maybe, more is the pity.

In the true spirit of the training we had all received in the British Army, inter-regimental rivalry played an important part in establishing the *esprit de corps* which, over the centuries, has been such an integral part of the fortitude and success of the Officer Corps. SAF was no exception. We had inter-Service rivalry between the Army, SOAF and the fledgling Navy. Within the Army units the competition was fierce and friendly. The Desert Regiment was recently formed and trying to find its own character and assert its authority. The main rivalry was between NFR and MR. Colonel Mike Harvey had Command of NFR and seldom has there been a more competitive or competent commander. An MC in Korea, judo Black Belt and a stubborn Infantry streak made him a formidable adversary. He trained his Regiment to the highest standards and they were very much in the mould of what was preferred by CSAF - lots of basic infantry skill training, long days on the range and nothing left to chance. Peter, in his own way, was equally competitive, but nothing would divert him from the fact that life was fun and he encouraged a flair in MR that was the envy of all. He had some very sound Infantry and Royal Marine Officers, but he was also prepared to accept the spirited cavalry officer to his command. Patrick Brook, Ranulph Fiennes, Nick

Roberts and Richard Kinsella-Bevan were quickly and quietly absorbed into the Regiment. Richard John, ex-Scots Greys, was a seasoned warrior but Peter encouraged them all to bring to the task a slightly lateral thought process. It made the Regiment somewhat unpredictable and it was not solely because the officers concerned had little training for the task but simply that they had been brought up in a different environment.

Peter established an *esprit de corps* which is hard to imagine or emulate. We were thoroughly professional and bound by the most extraordinary loyalty to each other and particularly to him. Dhofar was our battleground and the centre of all our thoughts, pains and anguish. It was not, however, the 'be all and end all' of our lives.

When in the North we trained hard but we had much fun as well. The few girls that were there, two American nurses and a secretary from Petroleum Development Oman (the beautiful and promiscuous Monica), longed for our arrogant return from the mountains of Dhofar. Our parties were legendary. Friday lunch at the Beach Club, water skiing and endless efforts to entertain all and sundry served two purposes. Firstly, Peter charmed everyone and, secondly, we took advantage of it.

Christmas lunch on the beach, four thousand miles from home, Mummy and Daddy and our legion of girlfriends was an event of considerable administrative planning and ingenuity. Peter had arranged for local dignitaries to be entertained in the Mess tent and a Christmas flight from SOAF to deliver lukewarm mince pies, prepared in CSAF's private kitchen, and champagne.

14

Operations continued relentlessly and Peter began to implement his new strategy. The quality of Intelligence began to improve and, although there were a number of routes suitable for camel trains coming in from the Aden Protectorate, it was now possible to establish that these routes converged into two or three narrow defiles in the mountains and foothills south of Defa and to the north of the fishing village at Mughsayl.

It was decided that the static positions on the Jebel served only a limited purpose. Although they dominated the local areas, they also became targets for enemy action and our ability to patrol at long distance from these bases became less effective. With our own limited resources we could certainly dominate the Salalah Plain and its various strategic targets, but it was difficult to concentrate our forces in sufficient strength to take the battle to the enemy on the Jebel.

By now we could absolutely rely on the support of SOAF and, apart from monsoon periods, we always had one of the two dhows from the Sultan's Navy available for amphibious operations.

We had spent quite long enough defending our lines of supply — ie the Midway Road — against attack from the enemy and it was now time to reverse roles. In the previous few months the enemy was certainly appearing to be better trained, armed and commanded than in the past and it was vital to try and interrupt or slow down this process. Peter described the reasons for his change of strategy in a letter he wrote to Colonel John McKeown who commanded the Muscat Regiment in the 1970s and who wrote a dissertation on the Dhofar War and its significance.

"You correctly state that I decided to concentrate my limited resources on a line between Mughsayl-Idlewild. I think the reasons for this are important as, though I say it myself, they were the first beginnings of the coherent strategy which I believe guided the conduct of the war.

"Hitherto, SAF, myself included, had been diverting operations against likely enemy areas of the jebel trying to inflict damage on an increasingly numerous, mobile and widely-spread enemy. He, meanwhile, was anxious to force us to dissipate our very limited resources in penny packets all over Dhofar and to defeat us in detail. The ideal strategy, as with any guerrilla war, was to attempt to separate the enemy from his firm base – in this case across the South Yemen border. The ideal place to do this was, of course, where the tree line (and thus good cover for enemy movement) was at its narrowest – what subsequently became known as the Sarfait position. However, with only two companies and no helicopter it would have been quite impossible to maintain a position there at that time. I therefore decided to do it further east. The only position which could be maintained with the limited troops available – and still leave a reserve in Salalah – was the Mughsayl-Idlewild line, which was subsequently greatly reinforced and wired and became the Hornbeam Line. During the second half of 1969 MR static positions, patrols and ambushes severely inhibited PFLOAG re-supply to central and eastern Dhofar. Tim Landon, then SIO Dhofar, told me that the first enemy who surrendered in 1970 expressed amazement when this stop line was removed (when DR took over from MR in March, 1970) as they could get no significant arms, ammunition or food through to the East while it was deployed. This, of course, was the aim. If supply from the West could be prevented, the East would wither away."

From the new positions we continued to ambush the possible supply routes from South Yemen, and contact and incident were frequent. It was very much a blind man's war and we seldom saw the enemy, who would engage us at fairly long range and try and make good their escape before we outflanked them on the ground or were able to pin-point targets for our support weapons, mainly the artillery and SOAF.

The logistical support for these operations continued to be a difficult problem to solve. A combination of lack of water, the casevac problem and the fact that whatever food and ammunition we needed had to be back-packed, meant that the best laid plans would, for one reason or another, have to be curtailed. The solid foundations of the strategy did, however, mean that whatever limited operations we could carry out were certainly of considerable nuisance value to the adoo.

Oh, for helicopters.

Oh, for the SAS.

We knew eventually that support would come but, in the interregnum period, it was frustrating and somewhat demoralizing.

Through this difficult period Peter held us together and it was an example of fine leadership. His junior officers, who continued to bear the brunt of the operational burden and the privations this entailed, were not far from breaking point. It was a mixture of a certain rectitude about the morality of their chosen mission, the isolation of their position, the importance given to it and the almost constant long-range contact with an enemy, that caused some of our number nearly to crack from time to time. Peter was always most conscious of the strain and provided such a pillar of moral strength that we were able to continue. Just before cracking point, he would pull an officer out of the front line of operations and dispatch him to base, to Muscat or even occasionally Bahrein, on a seemingly important mission which was, with the value of hindsight, simply to give him a break from the strain.

The trip to Muscat was the most regular rest and recuperation facility and a couple of days attending a non-existent conference recharged one's batteries, not to say one's enthusiasm, in double-quick time.

I remember Patricia Purdon, CSAF's wife, who insisted on at least having breakfast with incoming officers on their return to Muscat from Dhofar, being surprised by the change she saw in her young officers. "They went down as boys and came back as men." It was so true.

It was difficult to describe but, for young officers suddenly to find that their years of training were actually turned into reality – with dead and injured comrades around them – was, as many historians have remarked in the past, an experience that is paralleled by few events in one's life. To be under fire at any age changes one's perspective for ever and builds an extraordinary relationship with those with whom one shares the experience.

The feeling of isolation from the reality of the outside world and the seemingly uncaring or disinterested attitude expressed at all levels of HMG and, for that matter, our brother officers in the UK, simply bound us all closer together. We felt somewhat insulted when Dennis Healey, the Defence Secretary of State, declared to the House of Commons that, for the first time since 1945, no British servicemen were involved in action anywhere in the world – an early example of being economical with the truth!

In late August, 1969, Rakhyut, a fishing village close to the Border, was overrun by the adoo. It had only been guarded by a few askars and no attempt was made to recapture the village. The event was confusing. Certainly the Governor was arrested, tried, convicted and shot, but some reports gave the number executed as up to eighty and that most of the males were massacred.

MR was simply too stretched to try and recapture the outpost. It would have been possible but the resources to hold it were just not available.

In order to bring in supplies from the North we continued to spend inordinate amounts of time opening the Midway Road. While our ability to gather worthwhile Intelligence was improving so was that of the adoo. Despite our efforts to divert their attention by diversionary operations in other areas, the adoo almost always knew of our intentions. It was hardly surprising. A convoy of sixty vehicles leaving the North, which had to follow a certain route and took some four days to complete the journey, was not an event that could be carried out without some sympathizer getting wind of the arrival at Midway. Wireless silence was always observed but there was some pretty sophisticated jamming and intercept equipment in South Yemen, supposedly of East German origin, which was used to the adoo's advantage.

Gone were the days when the Midway Road could be opened by a company strength operation; it was now a battalion group task and Brigadier Corran Purdon recalled an occasion when he joined Peter Thwaites on a road opening operation:

"We had a battalion HQ and three rifle companies clearing from the plain towards Midway, and two rifle companies (B Company MR under Roger Brown and A Company NFR under David Shillinglaw, both splendidly aggressive leaders) clearing down towards us. We had the fire support of two 5.5 inch mediums and three 25 pounders, and air support from SOAF Strikemasters... We put in a battalion attack early on from our main body, and altogether I think we put in four more attacks at company or above strength before we met Brown and Shillinglaw's companies at Aqabat Jasmeen."

The escalation of the war was apparent for all to see and CSAF obtained the Sultan's acceptance that another company be permanently attached to the Dhofar Battalion group. At their frequent audiences with the Sultan both CSAF and Peter Thwaites encouraged him and finally persuaded him that he renew his request to the British Government for further support. Concern was escalating in Whitehall and the time was right to press home the argument.

We all felt that, given support, particularly helicopters, we could defeat the enemy, but, with the value of hindsight, this was probably optimistic. SAF did not realize it was outnumbered. Reliable sources later confirmed that PFLOAG had two thousand fighters in Dhofar, supported by three thousand militia. They had complete control and support of the Jebali population, certainly those living on the Jebel. It mattered little whether this was by conviction or coercion. The adoo were utterly ruthless towards any dissenters and executions and torture were frequent. SAF did not have the resources to provide the protection required for those who wished to remain loyal to the Sultan. Equally we did not have the Sultan's support for developing a 'hearts and minds' approach to the Jebalis' problems.

In January, 1970, Taqa, a small fishing village on the edge of the plain was attacked by a determined group of fifty adoo, supported by mortars and rockets. Peter counter-attacked and relieved the garrison, but sniping continued, particularly from the Mosque. Hearing of the affray, the Sultan insisted the Mosque be destroyed, but Peter resisted this order in a continuing effort not to further alienate the Jebalis. Sudh, another fishing village – but isolated far to the east of Salalah – was captured in March, 1970, by the adoo. A determined counter-attack by MR, which consisted of a night amphibious landing supported by SOAF, recaptured the village but it could only be a temporary victory as resources to hold Sudh simply were not available.

Concurrent with this activity, the enemy increased their attacks on

RAF Salalah and the Plain positions. It was perhaps a mistake by the adoo to target the RAF station as this simply drew HMG into a position where it had to do something. To withdraw was never an option as the Sultan would almost certainly have countered this threat by insisting on a withdrawal from RAF Masirah which, by now, was of increasing importance to the strategy of the West.

Direct support was given to RAF Salalah and mortar-locating radar was provided and further personnel from the RAF Regiment to provide close protection to the airfield.

Colonel Johnnie Watts, Commanding Officer of 33 SAS, appeared to follow-up on the appraisal for limited SAS support that John Slim had started eighteen months before.

The rebellion was now designated a war – but then it had been for some time.

Desert Regiment appeared from the North to take over from the Muscat Regiment and Peter Thwaites handed over command and left MR and SAF. I am sure he was relieved to have a break from an extended and hectic period of operational command. It was, however, a sad day and the end of an era. He had had the most profound influence on us all.

15

Before Peter Thwaites left Dhofar, the criticism of the Sultan's attitude to the war and particularly the Jebalis' role in it, increased considerably. His Highness was thought by many outside, and for that matter inside, observers to be too reactionary and almost feudal in his outlook.

The oil was beginning to flow and most now considered that the resulting revenue should be used to re-equip and expand the Sultan's Armed Forces. Hospitals and new schools were needed and the apparent lack of any real progress was perceived to be the fault of the Sultan.

Many officers had experience of guerrilla warfare in Cyprus, Malaya and Borneo and the complete lack of any coherent 'hearts and minds' policy was anathema to them and blame was laid squarely on the Sultan.

The endless hours of idle chatter concluded that it would be in everybody's best interest if the Sultan abdicated in favour of his son, Qaboos. Some even suggested a *coup d' état.*

Rumours began to circulate and morale began to suffer. Brigadier Corran Purdon reacted fast and ordered his Commanding Officers to put a stop to all this idle speculation, quite rightly pointing out that the loyalty of both contract and seconded officers was to the Sultan. It was not our role to become involved in playing politics.

Peter Thwaites, as one might imagine, was fiercely loyal in his support, and all ranks of the Muscat Regiment, particularly the officers, were left in no doubt as to the correct course of action.

It was not known to CSAF or Peter that events were being orchestrated many miles away in Whitehall. The strategic importance of winning the war in Dhofar and stopping any further progress by PFLOAG had finally been established.

The events that followed continue to be shrouded in secrecy but the eventual *coup d' état* was, in the belief of many of those whose opinions were of value and integrity, a pretty shoddy piece of British diplomacy.

On 23 July, 1970, Qaboos, Said bin Taimur's only son, forcibly deposed his father. The announcement was met with rapturous acclaim by Dhofaris and Omanis.

The financial resources were luckily now available to expand SAF in both numbers and equipment. The international community was now prepared to provide both covert and direct support. The SAS arrived, 'hearts and minds' became a priority, and gradually the Dhofaris' support for the new Sultan was harnessed.

The war was eventually won in December, 1975, but not before it had escalated further and the efforts of SAF had been considerably enhanced with direct support from the UK, Iran, Jordan and Saudi Arabia.

What had been achieved by Peter Thwaites in his period of command of the Muscat Regiment, and indeed CSAF – Mike Harvey and subordinate officers – had laid the foundation of this later victory.

With little doubt, that period was the most fulfilling and exciting in the annals of the history of SAF. It was the leadership of the British officers and the quality of it shown by Peter Thwaites that held PFLOAG at bay when so easily they could have forced home their advantage and established a stranglehold over the oil that the West so desperately needed.

GLOSSARY

[1]Bait is the Arabic word for house. The correct plural is buyoot.

[2]Tango — Fluorescent panels arranged in the shape of the letter 'T' (Tango) to indicate a target to the pilot.

[3]Adoo — Enemy

[4]This state of readiness meant that the aircraft were airborne within a few minutes' flying time of the ground troops but not visible to them — or to the enemy.

[5]Phosphorescent panel laid on the ground to indicate to the pilot the position of friendly troops.

[6]"Peace be with you" — "And on you, be peace."

[7]Egypt, Cyprus, Malaya, British Guiana, British Cameroons.

[8]Later Major-General M. J. H. Walsh, DSO.

[9]*Having been a Soldier.*

[10]Shemag — Arab head-dress, usually kept in place by an 'agal' a circle of cord around the scalp.

[11]Sangar — A defensive position made of stones, usually circular in shape.

[12]Gaysh - Colloquial Arabic for 'The Army'.

[13]M'arif — I don't know.

[14]One came to accept this yardstick when planning operations; in fact it was vital when trying to compute the time it would take to march a battalion into a certain rebel area, up or down perpendicular routes. Only when planning artillery support did horizontal distances matter.

[15]A long, flowing, cotton garment. Worn over dishdash.

[16]Well done! Sambo.

[17]Fadl — party (literally "favour").

[18]PFLOAG documents subsequently discovered.

[19]*Siyassi* — Intelligence Agent.

[20]"The oil company is marvellous!"

[21]Literally — "red".

[22]Askars — Omani equivalent of "Dad's Army".

[23] *Fiendeen* — The corrupt Arabic plural of "fiend" which Patrick Brook had invented as a codename for Fiennes' platoon.

[24]For this and his gallant action in the previous conflict, Mohu Gazzi was awarded a posthumous Gallantry Medal, the Sultanate's highest award for bravery.

[25]For those who served later in the Dhofar Campaign, this system of linked positions was much reinforced and was subsequently called Leopard Line.

[26]Special Operations Executive.

THE MUSCAT REGIMENT – 1969

OFFICERS AND NCOs

BN HQ

Appointment	Rank	Name	Regt/Corps
CO	Lt Col	P T THWAITES, jssc,psc	Gren Gds
2iC	Maj	J M COOPER, MBE, DCM	Late SAS
Adjutant	Capt	D M BAYLEY	Late R Sussex
IO	Capt	P C B BENNETT	Late 12 Lancers & 22 SAS
A/Adjutant	Lieut	GHULAM RASAL	
RSM	WO1	MAN NEK BAKHAT	
Chief Clerk	Sgt	SHAH DIN	Late Pak Inf
Pay Sgt	Sgt	BASHIR AHMED	Late Pak Army

HQ COY

Appointment	Rank	Name	Regt/Corps
Coy Comd	Maj	D E FOULDS	Late RA
Coy 2iC	2Lt	KARIM BUX	
OC Recce Pl	Capt	Sir R TWISTLETON-WYKEHAM FIENNES Bt	Scots Greys
QM	Capt	C ROGERS	1 RHF
MTO	2Lt	AYAZ PULLAN	
RSO	2Lt	KABIR KHAN	Late Pak Army
RQMS	RQMS	TAQI HUSSAIN	Late Pak Army
MT SGT	Sgt	NAGMAN PULLAN	
Signals Sgt	Sgt	MOHD HUSSAIN	
Pnr Pl Comd	SSgt	JAN MOHAMMED	
CSM	WO2	MOYD SALEEM	
CQMS	CQMS	GHULAM MOHD	

'A' COY

Coy Comd	Maj	R S JOHN	Scots Greys
2iC	Capt	M O'SULLIVAN	Late Inniskillings
Coy Offr	Capt	T D THOMPSON	RM
Coy Offr	2Lt	ABDUL WAHID	
CSM	WO2	PIR MOHD	
CQMS	CQMS	HIDAYAT ULLAH	
No 1 Pl Comd	SSgt	SAID SAIF	
No 2 Pl Comd	SSgt	SAIF HAMED	
No 3 Pl Comd	SSgt	JAN MOHD	
No 4 Pl Comd			
Mor Sec Comd	Sgt	MOHD JAN	

'B' COY

Coy Comd	Capt	H E AFFLECK GRAVES	RM
Coy 21C	Capt	P M R BROOK	Blues & Royals
Coy Offr	Capt	R V C BROWN	Late Royal Fusiliers
Coy Offr	Lt	KHALFAN SALIM	
CSM	WO2	SAID MOHD	
CQMS	CQMS	KHUD BUX	
No 5 Pl Comd	SSgt	HAIDER PULLAN	
No 6 Pl Comd	Sgt	MOOSA HASSAN	
No 7 Pl Comd	SSgt	HAMED MANA	
Mor Sec Comd	Sgt	MUBARIK	

'C' COY

Coy Comd	Maj	S F SLOANE	A & SH
Coy 2iC	Capt	J M G SHERIDAN	RM
Coy Offr	Capt	R D KINSELLA-BEVAN	5 Innis DG
Coy Offr	2Lt	JAN MOHD	
CSM	WO2 PIR	MOHD SHERAN	
CQMS	Sgt	MOHD KARIM	
No 9 Pl Comd	SSgt	SALIM SHEIKHAN	
No 10 Pl Comd	SSgt	MOHD ALI	
No. 11 Pl Comd	SSgt	KHUBA BUX	
Mor Sec Comd	Sgt	BAHRAM BALACH	

BRITISH SECONDED AND CONTRACT OFFICERS AND NCOs KILLED IN THE DHOFAR WAR, 1965-1975

Captain A. W. Woodman, late Royal Marines
Captain H. B. Emslie, late Royal Marines
Captain E. G. C. Vutirakis, late Special Air Service Regiment
Lance Corporal P. Reddy, Coldstream Guards
Flight Lieutenant A. W. Macdonald, late Royal Air Force
Flight Lieutenant J. Wynne, late Royal Air Force
Captain I. E. Jones, Royal Army Medical Corps
Captain S. J. Rae, Royal Marines
Captain M. R. A. Campbell, Coldstream Guards
Flying Officer D. E. Moore, Royal Air Force
Sergeant J. S. M. Moores, Coldstream Guards
Major T. E. F. Taylor, Royal Green Jackets
Trooper C. Loid, Life Guards
Lance Corporal D. R. Ramsden, Parachute Regiment
Gunner M. J. Martin, Royal Regiment of Artillery
Captain R. H. Jones, late Royal Welch Fusiliers
Corporal T. Labalaba, Royal Irish Rangers
Trooper T.P. A. Tobin, Army Catering Corps
Major P. S. Wright, Corps of Royal Engineers
Flight Lieutenant M. J. Drybanksi, Royal Air Force
Flight Lieutenant B. G. Handyside, Royal Air Force
Lance Corporal A. Kent, Cheshire Regiment
Captain S. Garthwaite, Royal Irish Rangers
Major J. Braddell-Smith, late Lancashire Regiment
(Prince of Wales's Volunteers)

Captain N. C. T. Loring, Light Infantry
Flight Lieutenant P. L. Davis MC DFC, late Royal Air Force
Captain W. N. Marshall, Royal Marines
Captain M. G. A. Shipley, Royal Anglian Regiment
Captain P. A. Mann, Queen's Dragoon Guards
Corporal D. C. Jones, Corps of Royal Engineers
Lance Corporal K. Small, Parachute Regiment
Private C. Hennessy, Parachute Regiment
Flight Lieutenant J. O. Heathcote, Royal Air Force
Flight Lieutenant R. Boyce, late Royal Air Force
Sergeant A. E. Gallagher, Royal Corps of Signals.

OPERATIONS REPORT

MR Gp
SALALAH
Dec '69

HQ SAF

MR Gp OPS APR — DEC '69

Reference: Your CSAF/1 of 091345D

1. Attached at Anx A are details of ops in Bn on two Coy plus str.
2. Anx B shows details of ops in Coy str with arty/SOAF Sp.
3. These are all "set-piece" ops. Normal Coy patrolling, ambushing and search ops are NOT incl — although these frequently had contact with the en and produced en or SAF cas.

SUMMARY

4. Out of 45 setpiece ops, 21 of which have been involved Tac HQ and two or more Coys. Contact was made with the en on 18 occasions.
5. Out of 45 major contacts with the en 36 were instigated by MR Gp as a direct result of offensive ops and 9 by the en.

RESULTS	EN	SAF
6.		
Confirmed kills	28	8
Unconfirmed kills	14	—
Confirmed wounded	11	17
Unconfirmed wounded	7	—
Prisoners	4	—
	—	—
Total out of battle	64	25

SYSTEM OF RECORDING EN CAS

7. En cas are not treated as "confirmed" unless:-
a. The en admit them on Aden Radio or in newspaper reports.
b. The bodies are recovered by SAF.
c. Two independent B2 int Sources report them (B2 sources are graded "normally reliable — Probably true").
8. All reports by B2 Sources are treated as "Unconfirmed" until corroborated by at least one other independent B2 Source, with the name of the cas.

MI/

Lieut Col Comdg

AWARDS OF THE SULTANATE OF OMAN, 1968-1970, DURING PETER THWAITES'S TIME

Name and Details	Award	Year
Cpl Allah Dad	Commd	1969
Pte Hammed bin Ali	Commd	1969
SSgt Hamed bin Mannah al Ma'amaria	WB	1969
SSgt Hamed bin Mannah al Ma'amaria	WSh	1970
Sgt Hassin Habitan	Commd	1970
Cpl Hassin Shambe	Commd	1970
SSgt Jan Mohammed	WKhM	1968
2Lt Khalifa bin Salim Sawalahi	WKhM	1968
Cpl Malang	CSAF Cmd	1968
WO2 Mian Nek Bakhat	WKhM	1968
SSgt Mohammad Ali	Commd	1968
Sgt Murad Jan	Commd	1969
Pte Murad Qadir Bux	Commd	1968
Cpl Obaid Mubarick	WB	1968
SSgt Obaid Mubarick	Commd	1969
Cpl Rasid bin Jumma bin Mashoud bin Rashid al Zidi	WSh	1969
Pte Rustan Mohammed Dad Karim	WKhM (G)	1969
WO1 Sed bin Mohammed bin Abdullah al Hossani	Commd	1970
Sgt Salim Mohammed	WSh	1968
SSgt Salim Sheikham	WB	1968
WO2 Sayed Taqi Hussain	Commd	1970
Sgt Siddiq Jumait	Commd	1967
Lcpl Sultan Mohammad	Commd	1969
Capt HE Affleck Graves — Royal Marines	Commd	1970
Maj PCB Bennett — Late 12 Lancers & 22 SAS	Commd	1970
Capt PMR Brook — Blues & Royals	WKhM	1970
Capt RVC Brown — Late Royal Fusiliers	Commd	1970
Maj RS John — Late Scots Greys	WKhM	1970
Capt RD Kinsella-Bevan BA — 5th Inniskillings Dragoon Guards	Commd	1970
Capt NA Lawrence	WKhM	1968
Capt JMG Sheridan — Royal Marines	Commd	1970
Capt SF Sloane — Argyll & Sutherland Highlanders	WB	1968
Maj SF Sloane	Commd	1970
Capt PD Southwood-Hayton	Commd	1968
Lt Col PT Thwaites — Grenadier Guards	Commd	1968
Lt Col PT Thwaites	WB	1970
Lt Col PT Thwaites	WKhM	1970
Capt Sir Ranulph Twistleton-Wykeham-Fiennes Bt — Scots Greys	WB	1970

Legend

Sultan's Gallantry Medal	WSH
Sultan's Bravery Medal	WB
Sultan's Distinguished Service Medal	WKhM
Sultan's Commendation	Commd

EXTRACT FROM A LETTER FROM
MAJOR RICHARD JOHN

Peter's tolerance and understanding of the various ways the nationalities that made up his 'Arabian Command' was second to none.

I well remember on one occasion A Company was tasked to move out on an operation at dawn and orders were given the previous evening by myself to my Baluch Company Sergeant Major and mixed Arab and Baluch platoon commanders. I normally arrived to inspect the company half an hour before moving off. On arrival that morning, to my surprise, not a soldier was on parade. I eventually learned that the Sergeant Major had had an argument with the senior Arab and he had suffered a loss of face. After an hour of my negotiations getting nowhere, I had to go and inform Peter, feeling, quite rightly, that he might be very angry. However, he well understood the 'face' problem and the sensitivity of it in Arabia combined with the consequences if not corrected. He just replied:

"Richard — I will cancel the operation and I have every confidence you can sort it out eventually."

We did — some twenty cups of Omani coffee and five hours later. The Company paraded for the operation the next day on time.

EXTRACT FROM
"A Sartorial Officer"
COLONEL JOHN MOORE

I first fell under the spell of Peter in 1961 having been temporarily posted to 1 Grenadier Guards for an Emergency Tour in the British Cameroons.

It was an unexpected delight to meet up again when I was posted to Oman in February, 1968. I was particularly fortunate as my job presented an excuse for frequent visits around Oman and Dhofar.

There life was real and earnest. My aim was to visit as often as possible, to learn first hand of their material needs and then endeavour to provide them. Such basics, given maximum emphasis under which Peter left me in absolutely no doubt, included footwear of any sort suitable to jebel bashing, a serviceable woolly pully and any form of battle ration. His command skills and administrative ingenuity were legend. One big problem on the jebel was air free drop re-supply of water to enable patrols to stay longer in arid areas. At the blunt end we tried everything from sealed kit bags to sewn-up goat skins as used by nomads. Light suddenly dawned. With the co-operation of Carlsberg and beer-drinking officers, the cans could be water-filled, frozen, re-packed and flung merrily out of a Beaver before its electrics were saturated. This, for Thwaites, was not enough. Surely the same principle could be applied to ghee tin flimsies with greater capacity and relatively less bulk? Sadly this was not to work as the flimsies, at mountain temperatures, took for ever to thaw and, when they eventually did, the taste was indescribable. Such were the logistical problems of a commander in 'undeveloped warfare'.

However, even in Dhofar, Peter maintained his sartorial individuality as was exemplified in his wearing of the shemagh. Not for him the flowing tails of a latter day Lawrence but infinitely more practical, and his unique method of wrapping to ensure personal protection, minimum hazards either in Landrover or Beaver and an undoubted signal to all that the Commanding Officer was present. It may not have been Ascot but it was the boss. I can picture him now.

I was so lucky to have his friendship. This is my tribute to a valiant soldier and a special gentleman officer.

EXTRACT FROM A LETTER FROM
MAJOR PETER RAVEN

When Peter took over command in Salalah, we were about to do a search and sweep operation on the jebel just west of Taqa. C Company did a night approach march up the escarpment from the South or sea-side, whilst A and B Companies swept down towards us from the North.

We had a 'cab-rank' of two Provosts on call overhead. Sometime in the middle of the morning my stops reported movement in the thick scrub and I could see indistinguishable figures moving towards us. I called in the Provosts, the first of which opened fire just as three men broke cover onto an open patch of ground and I realised from their uniforms that they were ours.

I called off the attack, but the leading Provost had hit a Company leading elements with a burst of MG fire, causing casualties.

Soon after, Peter came up to my position with his signaller and escorts. I briefed him as to what had happened — expecting a furious tirade — but all that he said was:

"Right, Peter. What can I do to help?"

I replied that we needed an emergency airstrip as close to the foot of the Jebel as possible. Immediately, he took the few men that I could spare, gathered up every cook, driver and bottlewasher he could find and disappeared back down the Jebel.

By the time we had concentrated and carried the casualties off the hill, Peter had cleared a strip and had positioned a Beaver for casevac.

Later, on return to camp, I was called to his quarters. Expecting the worst, I went in, was handed a glass of whisky with the words:

"You did what was right at the time, then rectified the error with dispatch. Now let us enjoy a drink together before dinner."

On our return from Salalah to Bid Bid, Peter decided that the Muscat Regiment needed smartening up for barrack duties and a Presentation parade ex Salalah. Only Peter could have produced a full team of Grenadier Drill Instructors who fully entered into the spirit of the occasion and, almost overnight, transformed a rather slipshod outfit into a very creditable drill-orientated Regiment. Expressions of amazement from all and sundry were simply met with a rather surprised raised eyebrow from Peter and a rather curt:

"Well, what else did you expect?"

What a super dedicated professional soldier and very human man.

EXTRACT FROM A LETTER FROM COLONEL KINSELLA-BEVAN

I arrived in the Muscat Regiment in early 1969 with much to learn, coming as I did from a cavalry regiment and moreover as a university entrant. Peter Thwaites' calm and thinking approach to problems was immediately most reassuring. Intelligence, ability and patent sincerity could fool the unwary into not noticing a powerful will and determination underlying the courtesy shown.

Never was his determination more evident than on LANCE, Colonel Peter's operation for striking at the heart of the adoo strongholds at the centre of their trans-border supply routes when it took great courage on Peter's behalf to extract us from the situation and arrange Maula Dad's return to base.

Peter was one of those leaders who minded, minded sincerely, about those entrusted to his care, thus generating a deep and lasting impression.

AN EXTRACT FROM A LETTER FROM
F.L. LOCKWOOD CBE

My contacts with Peter in Oman were in a staff rather than a field capacity and thus less relevant to *Muscat Command*, but my memories of the man are so warm that I would not want to miss the opportunity to write something and I hope the following contribution may make Jacqueline smile.

Peter and I had crossed paths in various parts of the world and in December, 1978, I was summoned by him to Sussex Street, having previously been telephoned to ask advice on how to hire the Banqueting Hall in Whitehall for a wedding.

What he had not told me was that it was for his wedding and it was not until Jacqueline opened the front door that I realized why nothing less than Inigo Jones's masterpiece would have been appropriate for that occasion. I should also have realized that I was about to be treated to another demonstration of Peter's style!

In response to a request for assistance in restructuring MOD Oman, several candidates had been mustered, of whom I was one, and Peter had the job of interviewing us. To this end he had arranged a friendly lunch for four, including the Duchess of St Albans, as my fellow guest, and Jacqueline. The two ladies found the subject of the rebuild of Wellington Barracks a very dull subject, preferring a more personal investigation of my CV. The Duchess refused to believe that I had been christened simply and uncompromisingly 'Fred'. "But what are you going to do when you go to the Palace?" said she. Peter, ever the good host, commiserated with my predicament which until then I had not seen as my most pressing problem!

Whilst I was thus regaled, the weather had taken an even icier turn and the streets were glassy. When we came to leave the Duchess and I fell, or more exactly slipped, into each others arms on the pavement and tottered off in a posture of mutual support. Peter's expression as he waved us goodbye remains a treasured memory.

Only such a man could have inducted someone into the service of MOD Oman with such style.

EXTRACT FROM A LETTER FROM MAJOR GENERAL CORRAN PURDON MC, CBE

I first met Peter Thwaites in late 1967 when I was commanding the Sultan of Oman's Armed Forces and he arrived to command the Muscat Regiment. His sincerity, charm, sense of humour and natural leadership made an immediate impact on all ranks. Peter took the war to the enemy, showing himself aggressive, fearless and tactically sound. Before Muscat Regiment returned to North Oman he had been decorated for gallantry. On subsequent tours he would win the Bravery Medal and the Distinguished Service medal. I personally witnessed his imperturbability and clear thinking under fire on a number of occasions. He set and achieved the highest standards, yet he made soldiering fun for everyone — except the adoo! We were close friends until his untimely death. I salute his memory.

INDEX